Dear, Sister

Greatness lives within you.

Awaken your Brilliance!

Use your gift to imagine, create, and

innovate.

Succeeding against all odds.

Thriving in your purpose.

Empowering yourself to be the change you

seek.

Making a difference to impact the world.

~Sincerely

Brittany Wilkins

Lyfe Engineering Coach

Letters to My Sisters in Engineering

Brittany Wilkins

SUCCESSFULLY INSPIRING ENGINEERS

Letters to My Sisters in Engineering is a work of non-fiction. To protect the privacy of others, certain names, organizations, and events have been changed and condensed.

Successfully Inspiring Engineers Paperback ISBN: 978-1-7358647-0-9

eBook ISBN: 978-1-7358647-1-6

Book Design By: Abdullah Al Maruf

Cover Design By: Connect Branding

Edited By: Candace Shabaka

www.brittanywilkinsspeaks.com

Library of Congress

Cataloging in Publication Data

Library of Congress Control Number: 2020919290

Manufactured in the United States of America

For my family, one of my greatest blessings:

Mom

Sabbrina, William, Christina, Aaron Sr.

Rodney, Alana, Bryanna, Celeste, Danica, Chris

Korey, Tobias, Danaysha, David

Aaron Jr., AJ, Antwon, Amari

Yazalina, Starr, Joann

Contents

Preface

Engineering is a career path pursued by many but traveled by few. It is all a matter of whether one is willing to go the distance. I have come a long way on the journey to becoming an engineer. Despite the challenges, setbacks, and disappointments, I was determined. I had a dream. I had a dream to impact the world and make it a better place. Engineer a world that created the future technological advances that would move our society forward. It was my persistence that enabled me to live out my dream of becoming an engineer. I love driving down the highway, seeing the many different automobiles that I and other engineers have contributed to the automotive industry by designing processes, products, and procedures that make cars more safe, green, and connected to your smart devices.

I have come this far to realize that my dream feels empty and lonely, like something is missing. Then it dawned on me. YOU are what is missing from the field of engineering. Every time I look to my left and right,

I see very few women working alongside me in the engineering field. Only 13 percent of engineers are women in the workforce. The women who make up the 13 percent don't look like me. I questioned how come there aren't more black women. Where are my sisters in engineering?

Women are less likely to be found in STEM jobs, and that begins well before wages have any significant impact on a student's assessment. The numbers tell the story. According to the American Society for Engineering Education, "20 percent of Bachelor's degrees were awarded to women in engineering and computer science." "6 percent of Bachelor's degrees in engineering were awarded to women of color." Women are underrepresented in all engineering and related jobs. Women hold less than 25 percent of all the STEM jobs in the United States. The more I began to think about the issues and solutions needed to help more young women succeed in STEM, the more I realized that I have to be the solution. A solution that encourages you and other young women to succeed personally and professionally. The level of success I have obtained is meaningless if I am not reaching back to help others. The trials and tribulations happened to me, but not for me. This journey is no longer about me. It is about helping the next generation of aspiring female engineers. One of my favorite quotes reads, "Success is not about what I accomplish. It is about what I inspire others to do."

Dr. Martin Luther King's speech "I Have a Dream" has had a tremendous impact on my life. It inspired a dream from within. Just as he did, I too envision a different type of world. One that sees women at the forefront of engineering. The leaders of innovation. The change agents.

I have a dream for women in STEM to impact the world.

I am mindful that the path to educating, empowering, and elevating more women in STEM will not be easy, but it's worth the fight.

I have a dream today.

That young women will aspire to be scientists and engineers.

I have a dream today that women will defy the odds and rise above stereotypical barriers that try to hold them back.

I have a dream that girls will not buy into the notion they are not capable of excelling in math and science.

We shall overcome self-sabotaging thoughts that corrupt our minds and let doubt linger.

I have a dream to uplift and transform the minds of young women in STEM.

I have a dream that young women will define their inner brilliance and see the values within themselves to believe they can change the world.

I have a dream that the vision for this book would manifest to encourage you on the road toward your destiny.

In 2013, I began to live out this dream and began a speaking career to empower young girls to consider engineering as a career. I was hired by a university to be their keynote speaker for their women in science day program. In speaking with the Director of Engineering, I asked, "What do you want the talk to be about?" "How exciting it is to be an engineer," she stated. "I can share my story about success and failure." She said no. "Don't talk about your failures; this should be inspiring." "I wouldn't be here if it were not for my failures." "Brittany, I understand, you have an amazing testimony. I just want you to share a part of it. The other part you can talk about different engineering disciplines." I committed to her requests. There I stood speaking about all the glamorous things about engineering.

"Do it and you will go far," I told the girls. The room was a sea of white faces, with only one black girl. My employer had partnered with a local nonprofit organization. The Vice President of our company asked me to speak on my career experiences being an engineer. We were also asked to give a company tour. The agenda was to talk about the highlights of our job roles. I was to give the presentation on the role of an industrial engineer. Our component engineer gave the presentation on her role of being a mechanical engineer. Our hybrid engineer gave the presentation on his role as an electrical engineer. Our Vice President and Director sat in on the meeting.

Too often we sell success without the process. During the session, a young man asked about what obstacles we had faced, what we had failed at. Just as I was opening my mouth to prepare to answer, the Director of Engineering interjected and gave the politically correct answer: No job role is perfect, but our engineers find a way to get it done. Another speaking opportunity and I could only tell half the story. There were eight students that showed up that. Only one was a black girl.

We had given the students a tour of the facility. The

tour consisted of showing our wireless charging lab. The purpose of this lab was to develop a technology to charge an electric vehicle. This lab was restricted, which meant it was off limits. This was the one lab where my badge did not work. It was the second time I had been in the lab. First time was during my interview. Next we showed the students technology similar to Google Glasses. A worker would wear these glasses to assist in building a wire that goes into your car. No engineers were working on this. This was not part of the work our component engineer, electrical engineer, and I were working on. The Information Technology department was developing this product. Again it was all about the highlights, looking at all the cool stuff you could do as an engineer. I was standing there wishing that one day I could work on the cool stuff.

My college chemistry professor had asked me to speak on a career panel. The panel featured a nurse, teacher, doctor, gynecologist, and myself. Great panel of speakers with powerful testimonies of success stories. A mother in the audience had asked me what trials I faced majoring in engineering. I looked over at my chemistry professor before replying. I gave the politically correct answer. I wanted to tell the opposite side of success, but it was not what my chemistry professor asked me to do.

The dream hadn't been what I had hoped for. It didn't feel real or authentic to me. While doing speaking engagements, I noticed a pattern. There was only one or no black girls or young women in the audience. I felt God's calling on my life to educate, empower, and elevate young black women and girls. Praying to God, I said, "How do I reach these young girls?" I felt like I couldn't speak my truth. There was always some constraint placed on what I could or couldn't say when speaking to audiences about engineering. In my spirit, I felt like I was misleading people in a way, not fully able to educate people on the process of becoming an engineer and the many intangibles that come along with it. People don't know what an engineer really does and what they go through. This was confirmed as I was speaking with a mother and her daughter. I was at an engineering convention, recruiting on behalf of my company. The mother said to me, "My daughter wants to be a mechanical engineer. She wants to be hands-on." She further stated she didn't want to sit at a desk and be doing lots of paperwork. I found it interesting that the mother was speaking for the daughter. Also that her perception about engineering was off a bit. Mechanical engineers do design products and are hands-on, but there is so much more to than tinkering with toys all day.

It was what her daughter had been exposed to that

gave her this narrative. I understood why they thought like this, because it's how we sell engineering to attract people to consider a career. I had some accountability in this because it was the narrative I spoke about. There is always more to narrative that is left untold. In recruiting future engineers, it bothered me to learn that there were young women who knew nothing about engineering. At this same convention, I met a girl who was a sophomore in college. She had just discovered what engineering was. She had asked me for my advice on which engineering major she should declare. Her additional questions centered on life after college. She wanted to know what it was like working in Corporate America. I told her it would take days for me to explain working as black woman in engineering. Keeping in mind that I was representing the company, I couldn't get into the details. My colleagues were listening to our conversation.

One step at a time, I told her. Focus on school first. Many women go through school, earn their degree, and begin a career in engineering. They work so hard only to realize engineering is not for them. An article published by University of Wisconsin, "Stemming the Tide: Why Women Leave Engineering," states "*30 percent of women who have left the engineering profession cite organizational climate as the reason.*" This is the truth I wanted to speak about, but never had the opportunity to do so. Organizational climate and the politics always get left out of the narrative. It's not right to build women's confidence up to pursue engineering only to have it broken by the system.

Transparency will lead to better outcomes for women in engineering. A lot of what I share in this book are things I wish someone would have told me. I believe in keeping it real, as the truth sets us free. My mission to fulfill the dream and reach those I am called to serve led me to write this book. My intention for this book is share my truth so that you will come to learn about what it has been like for me being a black female engineer, things I have gone through, and experiences I've learned from. My story is not perfect. My hope is that you can draw inspiration that serves as a guide for you in pursuit of your dreams. More importantly, learn from my mistakes. My guiding principle is each one teach one. Any knowledge gained is to be shared.

Introduction

A people without the knowledge of their history is like a tree without roots.

Marcus Garvey

Since 1828 engineering has been described as the art of directing the great sources of power in nature for the use and convenience of man. Engineering used to be the basic building blocks of roads, canals, buildings, bridges, and docks. As the world continues to grow, the engineering fields have evolved. New technological breakthroughs have emerged, such as virtual reality glasses, wearable devices, self-driving cars, and humanoid robots that can read the emotions of humans. The greatest breakthrough has been the inclusion of women in the STEM fields. Women have begun and continue to reshape the field of engineering. In 1958, Mary Jackson became the first black female engineer at NASA. She devoted her career to developing reports for NASA. Her greatest accomplishment was helping women get STEM positions at NASA. Space missions like the

1969 moon landing would not be possible without Katherine Johnson's calculations. We would be lost on our road trip destinations if had not been for Dr. Gladys West, who played an instrumental part in programming the mathematics and calculations for a complex computer that we now know as the GPS. What remains to be seen is the increased representation of black women in STEM.

Diversity is missing from engineering. We need diversity of thought in the world to face new challenges in the science and engineering enterprise system. Where there is no diversity, there is no innovation. It is through diversity that innovations are born. Birthed are innovations that change the landscape of how we function and operate in society. If we do not do our part in helping to reduce the achievement gap for women of color, the United States will continue to struggle to compete with its global counterparts. As engineers, we strategize to develop new products and processes. It baffles me that we can't solve the problem of lack of black females working in STEM. It's a complex problem with many variables. According to the author of *Blacks, Science, and American Education*, "It is obvious that there are few black scientists because there are few blacks in graduate science programs, there are few blacks in graduate programs due to lack of encouragement and knowledge."

I believe the issue goes deeper than being able to perform well in mathematics and science. We can't self-identify in this field because we are not being taught the history of blacks in science. We have lost a wholeness of our history. We can't relate to STEM if we don't see or hear about the accomplishments of African Americans who have contributed to the field. I grew up in a public education system where I was mis-educated to believe that the African culture did not exist. In my history classes there was never any mention of African civilization. In one class a teacher told a group full of African-American students that we had no culture. WHO AM I? I wondered. The history I learned was Columbus discovering America and Dr. Martin Luther King having a dream. Other than George Washington Carver, there was very little talk of black inventors and scientists. I had no knowledge of Benjamin Banneker, Lewis Latimer, or Percy Julian, who played important roles in the transformation of American science. During black history month I asked my teacher about African Americans in STEM. My teacher's response was "It's not part of the curriculum." Dr. Ivan Van Sertima, Africana Studies professor, said, "A great many of our people have no conception of where they come from, what is going on and where they are going." If we are to define the future, we must study the past. Our ancestors made a way for us to blaze new trails in science and engineering. It is up to us to carry the torch where they left off.

What we have been told about our culture is only half the story. Many of us only relate to our history back to slavery. Our history is far greater than the March on Washington. Our history is far greater than Rosa Parks refusing to give up her seat. Our history is far greater than just the tune of We Shall Overcome. Someday is today. It's time for us to connect with our roots. If we have no history, we have no destiny. Understanding and learning the history of blacks in science and engineering is one way to self-identify in the field. I came to learn about the history of blacks in science by being introduced to it by a historian. The process of self-education began for me. It's amazing what you learn when you seek to uncover knowledge not previously known.

Here I would like to introduce you to some blacks in science. My goal is that this introduction will broaden your horizons. At the end of this book a list of recommended reading is provided for you to further explore.

ᛩ

Historians refer to it as the lost sciences of Africa. It is where we begin to learn and debunk myths about African Americans' role in mathematics and science.

Myth #1: African Americans played no role in the development of civilization and technological sophistication. History tells us that between 1,500 and 2,000 years ago, Africans living in Tanzania produced carbon steel. This was achieved through pre-heated force draft furnaces in which the temperature achieved roughly 1,800°C, some 200° and 400°C higher than the highest reached in European cold blast bloomeries. A bloomery is a type of furnace used widely for smelting iron from its oxides. The process for steel smelting during this time was well advanced, as they made steel through the formation of iron crystals rather than solid particles as seen in European smelting. Carbon steel is used in our society today for the development of buildings, infrastructure, tools, ships, automobiles, machines, and appliances.

Myth #2: African Americans are not good in mathematics. African Americans' use of mathematical concepts and principles goes back more than twenty thousand years. Archeologists discovered a carved bone, the Ishango bone, used by hunting and fishing societies.

Microscopic examination revealed notches on the bone that suggested a knowledge of multiplication by two and prime numbers. Mathematics was used by the Egyptians to construct pyramids and temples. The Egyptian value of was 3.16. We now know to be equal to 3.14. Our ancestors did have knowledge about mathematics and used it in many applications.

Myth #3: African Americans have no knowledge of science. Much credit has been given to NASA on the world up above. It was a world that was first understood by the Dogon of West Africa. For centuries, astronomer priests had knowledge of the solar system and of the universe. They knew the rings of Saturn, the moons of Jupiter, and the spiral structure of the Milky Way galaxy in which our planet lies. This led to two French anthropologists dedicating their lives to studying the dogon and acquiring all information they knew. The dogons were the only ones who knew the mystery of the Sirius star system. Sirius B star is small and invisible to the naked eye. The dogon knew this star and could map out its trajectory around Sirius A.

This brief insight shows the role those before us have played in contributing to STEM fields through their knowledge and use of it in their everyday lives.

ф

So commonly we continue to hear that minority women can't succeed in engineering. There have been women who pioneered the way for us, showing it is possible. Beverley L. Greene was the first African-American woman architect. She helped design many of the buildings at New York University. Jennie Patrick became the first African American woman to graduate with a Ph.D. in chemical engineering, in 1979 from MIT. Christine Darden was the leading NASA researcher in supersonic and hypersonic, with expertise in the area of reducing sonic boom. Annie Easley was a computer scientist, mathematician, and rocket scientist. She was a leading member of the team that developed software for the Centaur rocket at NASA, one of the first African Americans in her field. These women and many more faced far greater challenges in their day. They overcame the obstacles and pioneered the way for us. Because of them, WE CAN achieve great things in the field of engineering. Where will your place be in history? It's time to pave a new way for future generations.

PART I

My Journey to Success in STEM

Chapter One

Defining a Career

I was born in Youngstown, Ohio, to a single mother of five children. I believe I was born on purpose, for a purpose, and with purpose. Within me lay seeds of potential and greatness. Within those seeds lay dreams of hope to do the impossible. Inspired to achieve goals, I was filled with courage. Growing up, I didn't quite know how I would do it. I heard that where you are from determines who you will become. I didn't buy the lie. I am from a city of broken dreams and lost hope. When the steel mills shut down, gone were the days of living for a purpose. People took great pride in working for an honest living. I'd hear the Baby Boomers speak of times when Youngstown was the place to be. Growing up, I saw a different community.

I saw a community where not many aspired to do or become much.

I saw a community where becoming the neighborhood drug dealer was an aspiration.

I saw a community where settling for welfare checks and government cheese was the norm.

I saw a community where the only motivation for the day was getting high and that "fix."

I saw a community where young women thought of themselves as just being somebody's baby momma. Becoming a teen mother was popular.

I saw a community where getting a quality education was an afterthought. School was just a place to attend to be taught, but not educated.

I saw a community where not many people made it out. I understand what the bumper sticker phrase "STUCK IN OHIO" meant.

I chose to look beyond, envisioning another life for myself. I didn't want to be just another statistic. One of my favorite movies growing up was *Sister Act II: Back in the Habit*. The main character is Sister Mary Clarence, played by Whoopi Goldberg. There is a scene in her music class where she says to her students, "If you want to go somewhere and you want to be somebody, you better wake up and pay attention." Those words stuck with me all throughout my childhood. I wanted to be more, to make a difference and change lives. I wanted to be the change I hoped to see in the community.

More important, I wanted to write a different legacy for my family. Growing up on the upper Northside of Youngstown was a struggle. I knew of my father, but didn't know my father. As strong and independent as my mother was, I could see at times the burden was too much to bear. It seemed as though we were living beyond our means, not being able to pay bills. It is never a good feeling when the water department shows up to shut your water off. The worst part is everybody knows because they spray the sidewalk as indication that water has been shut off at that residence. I remember the days of sitting in the dark with lit candles because the electric bill was overdue. No cable television to watch my favorite shows. My brother Aaron and I pretty much wore hand-me-down clothes from older siblings or gently worn clothes from the Goodwill store. I was embarrassed at times to show up on the first day of school. While my classmates at our public school showed off their new uniforms, shoes, and backpacks, there I would be wearing last year's school clothes.

I grew up worrying about how my family was going to make it. I saw education as my way out. Seeing the paths my older siblings had chosen to take, it was not my intent to follow in their footsteps. I wanted my mother to have a sense of accomplishment that she raised one of her children to make something of her life. Just like many people, my siblings have fallen in the trap of getting caught up in the streets. My oldest brother, William, was persuaded to pursue a lifestyle of selling drugs. He became a dope dealer. My brother spent most of his young adult life behind bars for assaulting a police officer. My second oldest sister, Christina, got boy crazy in junior high school. At fifteen years old I watched her give birth to her first child. She would go on to have her second child a year later. The saying is true: History repeats itself. My baby brother, Aaron, followed the same path as our older brother. Never made it to his high school graduation. His only accomplishment to date is having four children by four different women.

I was destined not to let my home environment or my community shape the woman I would become. I often wondered if life would be any different if my father were around. I was under the impression that if individuals grew up in a two-parent household, they would be better off and have a chance at making it. My perspective would change when I saw firsthand my childhood best friend's brother get indicted for murder. My friend Katrina Stanford came from a good family. Her mother was a successful principal in the public school system. Her father owned a construction business at the time. They had everything. The guidance, support, and love of two parents weren't enough. Katrina's brother had chosen the street mentality as well. He was indicted on murder charges for killing his own best friend over a chain. This showed me that it doesn't matter what circumstances you come from; it's all a matter of choices that determine the outcome of our lives. Regardless of what I lacked, I refused to use it as an excuse. I told myself I was going to make it out of Youngstown. My drive to succeed fueled me.

Curiosity

Curiosity is defined as the strong desire to know or learn something. Growing up, I was one of those kids who asked a million and one questions. The world around me seemed complex. I wanted to know how and why things came to be. Everywhere I looked, I saw the world take shape in many different ways. For example, telecommunications revolutionize how individuals communicate. It used to be when you wanted to talk to somebody you had to pick up a landline phone, dial the number, and ask to speak to that individual. Then came pagers and two-way messengers, where it didn't matter if that person was home to receive a message. You paged that individual, left a message, and within a certain time period that person would call you back from wherever they were. What's popular today becomes obsolete tomorrow. Now cell phones are the primary way we communicate via various modes of talk, text, face chat, and tweet. I always wondered how companies knew what breakthrough technologies to come up with next? What was the driving force behind smaller phones vs. bigger phones? How telecommunications companies handle the networks that supply the mobile service? More important, I questioned who was behind these technological advances.

While riding along in my mom's car, I observed the major highway in our town at times would be under construction. Along the road there would be workers. I questioned who they were and what exactly they were doing, because the roads never looked any different. Until I noticed that the two lanes along the highway had expanded. I was curious to know how they calculated the width of the lanes to ensure cars wouldn't run into each other. I questioned how the weight of the vehicle affected the highways. How they made the decision to pave one side of the road and not the other. I would always ask those challenging questions nobody seemed to have good answers to. I guess I was an engineer in the making, always questioning and challenging the status quo of why things were the way they are. I also used to try to provide input on what needed to be changed, if I didn't like the way something was. Scientists and engineers don't just settle for things as they are. They are always looking for a better solution to improve things.

I really became interested in STEM watching the educational sketch comedy show *Bill Nye the Science Guy*. I learned how science and engineering were the fundamental core of how our society functions. From our foods to transportation and technology, we acquire information from engineering. I loved the wacky hands-on experiments he would do live on television. It was education beyond the classroom that took every day concepts, things people used, and showed the science behind them. I remember one particular episode when Bill talked about caves. Within the caves he mentioned formations called stalactites and stalagmites. These form slowly over time through the dripping and hardening of minerals. Bill showed the unique geological formations by doing a simple science experiment using Epsom salt, small glass jars, yarn, water, and a spoon. I thought this experiment was so cool that I attempted to make my own cave formations for my science fair project. The Science Guy definitely kept me engaged in science. I often wished he were my science teacher. I wanted to learn more about what engineers and scientists did and all the contributions they made to the world. Learning about engineering has been a lifelong process for me.

Today I still watch shows that teach and promote engineering. The science channel features a show *How's It Made*. The show leads you through a process of how everyday products such as apple juice, skateboards, engines, and contact lenses are manufactured. YouTube has enabled me to stay up to date on the latest innovations in engineering. I have learned how other women have contributed to engineering fields. Social media has opened doors, making information more accessible to us. I follow and engage with organizations dedicated to promoting STEM in communities.

<u>Exposure</u>

A teacher is one who not only educates but encourages those they teach to strive for greatness, helps those reach their fullest potential, and instills confidence in their students. Throughout my educational career, I've had many teachers who have played a part in my academic success. Very few have gone the extra mile to inspire me to pursue STEM as a career. The greatest challenge I faced growing up was never being exposed to STEM. I read about scientists and engineers, but never actually interacted with any.

This would all change once I entered high school. My biology teacher, Mrs. Branson, was an advocate for Women in STEM. She saw the potential in a couple of us and introduced us to careers that could lead to many opportunities. The local university, Youngstown State, hosted a Women in STEM career day. This career day was founded to provide positive role models and affirmative experiences in science to women, targeted toward middle and high school students. To this day, I remember what my first Women in STEM day experience was like. The workshop offered interactive laboratory demonstrations in various areas of science. STEM career day featured women from the community working within various science industries. The lab activities and demonstrations hooked me in. The WISE program is where I learned how to make my own perfume. The engineering behind perfume amazed me. The lab activity taught me that a chemical engineering degree could lead to a career in the cosmetics industry developing fragrances.

Silly Putty was one of my favorite toys to play with. Similar to playdough, it could be formed in any shape to stretch and bounce. As an experiment we were able to make our own variations of it as part of the one of the lab activities. I felt like a CSI detective as we got to experience the DNA forensics fingerprinting lab. Learning and doing science and engineering made it fun to be a part of. Women in STEM day was key to my learning about all the possibilities a STEM career could offer aspiring engineers.

It also exposed me to role models. I was inspired by the many stories I had heard of women making strides in the science and engineering industry. Hearing these women from different walks of life give their testimonies on how they pushed past adversity and broke barriers motivated me. The one thing these women all had in common was that they were from Youngstown. I knew right there and then that it was possible to dream bigger, reach higher, and not fall into the trap. Sitting there, I envisioned myself walking in the path many of them had chosen. Mrs. Branson took our group every year, which was very beneficial to me. Each year I gained new insight on what being a female scientist and engineer was all about. I had begun to learn the challenges women faced in these fields. I saw pursuing a career in STEM as my opportunity to become a part of history. My biggest takeaway was that the role engineers play in our society is critical. Engineers move the world forward. The true calling of an engineer is to serve humankind. Engineers are innovators who help, serve, solve, and make the world a better place. Engineers use science to discover, technology to invent, engineering to build, and math to solve.

Out of the six young women Mrs. Branson took to the WISE program, I was the only one who made the decision to major in engineering. I believe the seed was planted in me long ago. Mrs. Branson helped to nurture and grow that interest in STEM by providing me the opportunity to attend workshops to increase the underrepresentation of women in STEM. Youngstown State engineering school also had open house day, where engineering students showcased their class projects. Classrooms and labs were open and attendees got to see labs and equipment and to speak with faculty members. Again Mrs. Branson was the one who took our group to these open houses. For her to continue to invest her time in us showed me that she believed we had potential. The more I was exposed to the college atmosphere, the more I saw myself attending college. In the inner-city communities, not all have the opportunity to be exposed to STEM. I am grateful I had a teacher who cared about her students.

Inspiration

My mother had the greatest influence on me choosing engineering as a career. She once asked me what my top three career choices were. Career choice number one was engineering. I was a big CSI fan and the exposure to the forensics lab had me considering studying to become a forensic scientist as my second choice. And my third option was becoming a doctor. With any of these careers, the goal was for me to help people and make life better. All three career paths would enable me to do so. My mother said, "No matter what you choose to do, I believe in YOU." And then she gave me a binder full of pages about engineering. Its title page read, SO YOU WANT TO BE AN ENGINEER? A note followed at the bottom of the page, which said: *The sky is not the limit in engineering, you can go anywhere with an engineering degree. GO and leave your mark on the world.*

The resource provided was one step in the process of defining an engineering career. The second step was exploration. It began by studying the engineering fields. The pages outlined various disciplines including aerospace, chemical, computer, electrical, industrial, and mechanical engineering. The question was, Where would I choose to leave my mark? It was all about defining the "right" fit. It was about what seemed most appealing based on the engineering discipline description, typical work environments, average salary, geographic location, and job demand for each profession.

Industrial engineering is the field where engineers find ways to eliminate wastefulness in production processes. They devise efficient systems that integrate workers, machines, materials, information, and energy to make a product or service. The mindset in this field is, How can we make it cheaper, better, and faster? Industrial engineers don't build things, but make them better. Although mechanical engineering is the broadest discipline, industrial engineering is the most flexible. Skills learned in this profession can be applied to many different situations, from manufacturing to healthcare systems to business administration. Their versatility allows industrial engineers to engage in activities that are useful to a variety of businesses, governments, and nonprofits.

For example, industrial engineers engage in supply chain management to help businesses minimize inventory costs, conduct quality assurance activities to help businesses keep their customer bases satisfied, and work in the growing field of project management as industries across the economy seek to control costs and maximize efficiencies. I have a knack for looking at things not as they are, but as they could become. Our society is built and run off the production of good and services. Improving how to better streamline operations and assist individuals in their work environments is where I felt led. As I read the booklet my mother provided, this discipline made an impression upon me. I could see myself utilizing an industrial engineering degree in the area I was called to serve.

I would become the first engineer in my family. Second to graduate high school and college. My family told me to GO FOR IT! I am grateful for the binder my mother gave me, as it was a stepping stone on the path to purpose.

Knowing what one wants to do in life and preparing

to do it are two completely different things. The book provided by my mother only got me so far. It wasn't far enough. Taking a trip back down memory lane, there were some mistakes I made by not preparing sooner. The first mistake I made was not taking the right college-prep courses, working with high school guidance counselors to ensure course curriculum would be aligned with engineering school courses. If I were going into the medical field, biology, anatomy, and advanced placement would have been beneficial. More physics classes and advanced placement chemistry is where I should have been. I wasn't the best math student, but I managed to get by. Being the perfectionist that I was, I re-took algebra because I received a B. By doing this I missed the opportunity to take calculus. It would cost me later on in college.

The second mistake I made was choosing not to go to Choffin Technical Center my junior year. Beginning of junior year, students could attend vocational school to study a trade for the last two years of high school. The program offered hands-on experience and college credit toward a career. I declined to attend Choffin because it would have meant giving up honors courses. Also I would be away from my friends. I regret not at least giving it a try. Who knows what knowledge and experience I could have gained?

By far my biggest mistake was not researching and choosing the best colleges. The key is to find a college focused on preparing you for a STEM job. In deciding what college to attend, I should have considered the following:

Does the school align its STEM program with high-paying jobs in demand? Almost all schools offer STEM degree programs, but many institutions never connect their academic program to real-world job requirements.

Does the school have programs, resources, and relationships that help their students get jobs? Every college has a mission. Make sure the college of your choice is preparing you for success after graduation.

Are they attracting and supporting diverse students and faculties in STEM fields? There wouldn't be a need for diversity in STEM if it already existed. Diversity is critical to lead in a global marketplace. Make sure you understand whether the college of your choice is actively working to change the equation.

What resources are dedicated to supporting STEM student achievement and success? Many STEM degree programs have a weed-out system. It's key to know how the school will help you thrive within challenging courses to achieve long-term success.

STEMjobs.com is a great resource to begin your college search. This resource has listings of STEM colleges. It's best to visit your top college choices to get a feel for academic and social atmosphere.

It was foolish of me not to visit any colleges I wanted to attend before applying. Financial aid will also be determining factor in your STEM school of choice. I waited until my senior year to begin looking for ways to finance my college education. I didn't have much scholarship money at graduation. It was the primary reason I couldn't attend an out-of-state college.

With the rise of college tuition, many are continuing to be left behind. My advice is to start the scholarship search early. Waiting until your senior year, you will miss half the deadlines. If pursuing higher learning, my recommendation is to start in ninth grade. You may wonder where to look. My mother had given me a scholarship book for African Americans. I started writing letters to the organizations inquiring about funding. Many of the letters bounced back due to invalid addresses. The applications I did receive, I felt unqualified for. I was a great student and scholar-athlete but lacked overall leadership skills outside of school. Being well rounded with community involvement helps you stand out. Begin to look for local scholarships within the guidance department office.

Contact the financial aid offices of the colleges of your choice to see what they offer. The library jobs and careers section is another resource to utilize. Look online at websites such as NSBE.org (National Society of Black Engineers), PND (Philanthropy News Digest), news alerts part of the foundation center, and the many apps like Scholly. Google search engine will present you with options of where to search. The key is getting started. Apply for every scholarship you are eligible for. Tailor your application to the sponsor's goals. Before you begin writing any essays, outline all your thoughts. Talk about your impact and how it will affect others. When I wrote my scholarship essays, I always asked my English teacher to proofread. Social media will play a role in being considered for scholarships. It's important to keep a clean and professional profile across all platforms. Do not let funding for college prohibit your aspirations for attending, as your education can be funded through student loans. Student loans do have to be paid back. Be smart when estimating how much you need to pay for college. I encourage you to attend free financial aid workshops and courses that help students navigate the process.

Defining a career is a process. Take every opportunity presented to you if it will push you further. Do your homework on the area(s) that interest you. Lastly, prepare in advance. It's your future, so be proactive and take control.

Chapter Two

Overcoming Obstacles

My pursuit of a college degree began in August 2005 at Youngstown State University. The road to an engineering degree was anything but easy. Success does not come without obstacles. With every new adventure comes bumps in the road. These bumps are setbacks that will leave you feeling stranded with no hopes of making it to your destination. I faced trials and tribulations my freshman year of college. My academic performance didn't measure up to the level I'd achieved in high school. The college environment was different than what I was accustomed to. The environment was larger and more complex. It consisted of gender bias, social/cultural integration issues, and core curriculum courses with a weed-out policy in place. The program led many to fall flat. The engineering program exposed my weaknesses.

I will never forget the feeling of sitting in a classroom listening to a lecture for 50 minutes and not comprehending one thing the professor talked about. This feeling began in my pre-engineering course Engineering Drawing and Visualization. This class was intended to teach students to visualize objects given in orthographic views. This meant transforming 2D images into 3D drawings using isometric views of top, bottom, left, or right. How could I draw something I couldn't see? Spatial visualization was a skill I lacked. This critical skill is needed, as it's how engineers communicate their visions and ideas through the use of drawings and blueprints. Engineering drawing did not get any easier; it became more complicated. In discussing my issues with my professor, he asked whether Engineering was for me. I withdrew from the course.

It's not encouraging when you study all night for an exam only to receive a failing grade. I failed my first Chemistry exam. Dropping a second course was not an option, as it would reduce my full-time status. There will be times in life where situations and circumstances humble us. I had to swallow my pride to admit that I needed help. I joined a Chemistry study group offered by the center for student progress. With the extra help, I was able to make some progress. Failing test grades put me in a hole. Getting a passing grade in Chemistry was all dependent on the final exam. My Chemistry professor posted grades outside his office. The walk to Ward Beecher hall was dreadful. It was a sigh of relief to see that I'd earned a passing grade of a C. From the first test to the final exam, I bounced back strong.

Some courses were easier than others. Calculus I was the first class I failed. The final exam was nearly impossible. It was nothing like the quizzes or exams. The Math department had its own departmental exam it administered. I visited my Calculus professor in his office to discuss my grade. It hurt my feelings to know that I was close to passing the course. All I needed was one more point to earn a C. In talking with my professor, I wondered why he couldn't just give me that extra point. The lesson I learned from this experience was never expect things to be handed to you that you haven't earned.

I also failed Physics I, Engineering Computing, Calculus III, and Material Science. I was being weeded out; a C average seemed unattainable. There were days when I looked at the other majors and minors YSU offered. I thought back to my aspirations of being a doctor or forensic scientist. Those options did not appeal to me anymore. In some regards I felt stuck. Every day I questioned how I was going to pull through.

Failure is a bitter pill to swallow when you're used to succeeding. To me, anything beneath an A was not good enough. I cried and got upset when I received a B. So just imagine the emotion when those A's and B's turned into D's and F's. It was hard to come to terms with. I once was that National Honor Roll student, scholar athlete, and top 10 percent of my graduating class. Success was all I ever knew in academics. It was also where I placed my confidence and self-worth. There I was at the bottom looking out. Earning a college degree seemed so far away. The tunnel was dark with no light in sight. It led me to become depressed. It led me to sit in my room and cry. There were days I couldn't even make it back to my apartment. I cried on the way home. When I couldn't make it home, I cried in restrooms.

It didn't help that certain professors made things no better for students in the Engineering program. Many spoke discouraging words to the students. One professor even had the audacity to tell me that no matter how many times students complained to the dean, he was tenured and couldn't be fired. The system protected professors. The real educators saw the potential in me and wanted me to persevere. In the fall of 2006 while working at the YSU bookstore, I met my academic advisor for Industrial Engineering. I still hadn't declared my major, as I was trying to pull through first-year Engineering. We briefly spoke about the program and what it had to offer. I filled him in on where I was academically. He went out of his way to help me find a tutor for Calculus I. The second time around was much easier than the first. I had begun to catch on to the system. Many professors never change their lecture notes or exams. I took the same professor for Calculus 1 and memorized my old exams. But relying on my memory would cause me to stumble in other courses.

When I wasn't dropping courses, I surrendered by choosing to take a failing grade. My Engineering Computing teacher wouldn't let me give in. She taught the class at a very fast pace. The Engineering program consisted of students who came from good school districts in Ohio such as Boardman, Canfield, and Poland. Many of the students informed the professor that they already knew what she was teaching. A lot of material was not explained and skipped over. The public school system had failed me in more ways than one. I was so far behind. Every day felt like a race to catch up. Could

I compete with the best Engineering students? What do you do when your best isn't good enough? I visited my professor during her office hours to tell her I quit the course. She said the class wasn't difficult but that she knew how I felt. She told me the story of when she was a student in engineering school. By no means was it easy for her. At TCU she was the only female in her department. She proposed that I continue to show up to the class. Her recommendation was that she would give me until the end of the summer to complete the course. The extra time helped. I did as she instructed and received a B.

In Calculus III the same fate awaited me. Here I was faced with the decision to have to give up. My friend Melissa and I would sit in the library to study for hours for an exam we couldn't pass. I suffered from test anxiety. My mind would race throughout the first twenty minutes of the exam. It never felt like there was enough time. Again I sat in my professor's office telling her about my situation. I explained it made no sense to continue to show up to class. What good would it do me if all I ever received on an exam was a failing grade? My friend Melissa was in the same boat; she was about ready to give up. But we had missed the deadline to drop the course. My professor was not going to let us walk away and take an F. She gave Melissa and me until the beginning of the fall semester to complete the final exam. The grade we got on the final exam was the grade we earned for the course. I sweated through the final to get a C.

There will be those who are for you and those who will be against you. Through my journey, help was needed every step of the way. I looked to my professors as a source to help guide me. Many saw my efforts and committed to helping me. There was one professor, though, who insisted I give up. The story of every semester was failing at least two courses. The alternative was to drop courses by the withdrawal deadline. I will never forget that conversation with my professor. It was the turning point in my academic career. It shifted my focus and mentality because now I was out to prove a doubter wrong. My professor felt I shouldn't be in Engineering because to him I was struggling in easy courses. He called me lazy. Although my grades didn't show much, my efforts weren't the least bit lazy. I came to class every day, did the homework to the best of my ability, and studied for exams. The strength inside of me held back tears. I didn't want to break down in his office. We exchanged many words back and forth. The very last thing he said to me was "I am not going to give you anything." As I headed out I replied, "I wasn't asking you to." I couldn't believe he told me I didn't belong. I later found out that he had talked to my Engineering advisor about me. He told my advisor he didn't know if I was going to make it and questioned whether I should continue. Certainly I had thought some of those things myself. Every day I told myself, "You don't have what it takes to make it. Just accept the fact that you will never be good enough to major in Engineering." But hearing that negativity from this professor changed everything. I decided to continue on. I now had something to prove. The woman in the mirror was who I had to prove it to. Often the enemy is your inner self. Self-sabotaging thoughts had led me to be my own worst enemy.

I once heard an old parable about two wolves. A grandfather is talking with his grandson and he says, "There are two wolves inside of us that are always at war with each other. One of them is a good wolf, which represents things like kindness, bravery, and love. The other is a bad wolf, which represents things like greed, hatred, and fear." The grandson stops and thinks about it for a second, then he looks up at his grandfather and says, "Grandfather, which one wins?" The grandfather replies, "The one you feed."

I was managing my thoughts and emotions wrong, which led me to feed the bad wolf. If I was going to persevere in college, I needed to operate from a different state of mind. It was coming to terms with knowing that I didn't know it all, but I needed to remain teachable. Identify those weaknesses and work to address them. Dropping courses wasn't going to solve my problems of getting through the course. At some point I would have to take the class over again. It would only equate to me paying more money in tuition. I told myself to see it through to the end and live with the results. I was getting the same results because I was doing the same things. The definition of insanity. I didn't know how long it was going to take, but I was going to accomplish this. I told myself not to cry to give up but to cry to keep going. The journey will not always be sunshine and roses. It does not mean that the journey does not have purpose. The promise does not come without the process. The process was succeeding against all odds.

This incident with my professor woke me up. It just wasn't about going through the motions anymore. That very semester I was on the verge of a breakdown, but I broke through. It became by far my best semester. I didn't drop any courses. The result was the Dean's List and a $500 scholarship award. This was not the end of me facing my Industrial and Systems Engineering professor. I had no choice but to continue enrolling in his courses.

There were only three Industrial Engineering professors at the time. My perseverance turned a doubter into a believer.

The YSU Industrial & Systems Engineering chapter attended the regional Institute of Industrial Engineering conference at Purdue University. It's where other IE chapters in the region meet to learn and gain new insights into the field. The event kicked off with a social at one of the popular college bars. Socializing consisted of beer pong. Clubs and drinking were just not my thing. While the others participated, I sat alone at an empty table. Out of nowhere my professor walked over to me. He told me he was proud of me. It left me speechless. This was the same professor who had berated my intelligence. The environment we were in made me think he'd had one too many drinks. All I could say was thank you. He wanted to keep the conversation between us. I don't remember much about the conference. But I will always remember the changed way he spoke to me.

The whole experience felt like a wild roller coaster. Going up this steep hill trying to reach a level of achievement to move forward, only to reach the peak and come flying down the hill. Physics I lab proved to be another defining moment. The lab itself wasn't hard, but all students were required to take a fundamentals exit exam. If you didn't pass the exam, you failed the course. It didn't matter what grade you received on the lab assignments. Failure was staring me right in the face. To spend six weeks in a course only to get an F seemed unfair. Here I was the last person in the lab who had to pass it. I had failed to find a solution to my test-taking anxiety. It also didn't make any sense why the students had to take this exam. The real objective was never explained. The questions were not even related to physics. One question read, "How much does a penny weigh?"

Knowing how much a penny weighed wasn't common knowledge to me. Every day after class I took the exam. No exam was the same, different questions each time. In this case, memorizing did no good. I stood in the hall as I waited for the professor to grade my exam. She exited the class and entered into the head Department of Physics office. When she came back out, she told me she had tried to find ways to give me points. I needed a 21 to pass and I had a gotten a 19. Tears began to arise. I thought that was the end. My professor gave me a second opportunity to retest on a different exam. Lord, I know you wouldn't bring me this far only to leave me hanging—the prayer I said before starting over again. The second time I took it, my mind was more at ease. I had gotten into a little bit of a groove. I handed in the test and waited in the hallway again to await my fate. After five minutes I returned to the classroom. My last and final try was successful. I got a 23! I thanked my professor for not letting me fail. Trials and tribulations come to make us stronger. This moment definitely tested my faith. My faith to believe in performing under pressure. Testing of our faith produces perseverance. The lesson learned was that my will to succeed had to be greater than any test.

Time after time the will to succeed had to come from deep within. Many of the required courses were uninspiring. Physics I and II brought me no joy. They didn't inspire me to want to learn. I felt defeated three days a week for fifty minutes. The course syllabus read that a 40 earned a C. On a normal grading scale, 40 represents poor academic performance. In post-secondary every professor has their own grading scale and policy. When test time came around, students were allowed one index card with information. It was pointless. Majoring in STEM requires good problem-solving skills. Past learning experiences provided me all the variables to then pick the equation to plug into. Scientists have to think differently. In physics the professor expected students to derive the equations. The new level of thinking frustrated me. I would get irritated to the point where I would just hand in blank tests. I earned a D in Physics I. To me, D stood for determination, not defeat. Determined I was to earn a C in Physics II. I had the same professor. His lectures were just so dry and monotone. It was hard to understand concepts that I couldn't visually see. I had this habit of staring at the clock every class. My professor called me out on it one day, not understanding the material was the reason. The clock entertained me for 50 minutes. He recommended I sit front and center. At the time I didn't understand how that was going to help me. No matter where I positioned myself, I wasn't going to get the material.

How was I going to pass this class? I thought that maybe if I did the little things, it would show my professor I was trying to put more effort into his course. I didn't move my seat, but I stopped looking at the clock. I popped in during office hours to ask him questions. Instead of turning in a blank test, I worked the problems to the best of my abilities. Physics I compared to Physics II test scores progressively improved. I scored higher each time on the pop quizzes. My test score averages went from 10–20 to 25–40. On my second exam, I received a 40—the highest score I'd ever earned in Physics. In the end those minor things made the difference. I earned a C in Physics II, a milestone for me. It gave me the revelation that C's also get degrees. In my non-major courses, that was the new bar I set for myself. C stood for committed.

In college all (wo)men are not created equal. There were stereotypical attitudes and behaviors toward women in STEM. The longstanding belief has been that men are better than women at math, science, and the other skills that engineers need. Men will see you as inferior to them, as if what you have to contribute brings no value. At times my level of competence was questioned. My input was not taken into consideration for class projects and assignments. One case was in Engineering Computing. The professor required us to write a visual basic program. This was a collaborative project. It required me to work with a male student. Project ideas had to be approved by the professor before starting. My proposed idea was to write a visual basic program that enabled you to input standard work seconds for time studies performed on a repetitive job. My idea was shot down because it was too simple. My male colleague's idea was to write a visual basic program calculating standard entropy for a particular gas. "Entropy" in simplest terms is a process of degradation or running down or a trend to disorder. For example, when the ice in a glass of water in a warm room melts—that is, as the temperature of everything in the room evens out.

I received an A for the project. There was nothing that was done on my part to really take credit for. Several times I insisted and gave my input on the project. My partner refused to allow me to help him. I tried talking with him about a time to meet up, but no time was ever good for his schedule. He told me would handle everything. The only contribution I made was doing a process flow chart. Creating a pretty diagram with words. It felt as though he did not trust my ability to help him. How do you work with people who don't want your input? How do you sell your ideas so people see their value? This was my first taste of how it would be as a female engineer working in corporate life.

The same incident happened in my Methods Engineering lab. As an aspiring industrial engineer, methods engineering was a key fundamental course. Students were required to learn the basics of understanding job performance. The goal was to evaluate how the person does the job, looking at the following: environment, station layout, tools, and time it takes to complete each task. This is done to establish work standards and also find ways to improve the job. My professor had established relationships with local companies. To make the course more hands-on, he set up appointments for his class to go visit companies.

Roderick and I were assigned to do time study at one of the companies. We observed an operator assembling parts into a printed circuit board. I conducted most of the discussion with the operator. We recorded her so we could later break the job down into elements. The assignment required we write a report. This would be another battle, as Roderick resisted my help. I tried to convince him that my input was just as valuable since I'd spoken directly with the operator and understood the job from her perspective. He would hear none of it. I was zero for two in gaining the confidence of my peers. How could I build relationships with my peers to be seen as an asset?

It would have been so much easier to work independently. This is not how it works in the real world. Part of your job success will be to build relationships with your peers. The perception is that women don't comprehend well compared to our male counterparts. When you show intelligence beyond what is known, it can be intimidating to some. I wasn't going to dim my light to make others feel comfortable. These were early lessons learned in college. On the flip side, I had gained the vote of confidence of a few peers.

My attention to detail, research, organizing, seeing

problems before they occur, and coordinating big projects led some to believe in me. I excelled in project-based learning curriculum. Industrial Engineering senior capstone courses is where I began to stand out from the crowd. It took me four years to find my niche in Engineering School. These courses were two semesters. For one full year, students were required to design and build a production facility to produce a certain product. In the first few weeks, the professor gave the basic case scenario, inputs, and requirements. The biggest test came in choosing the right team. In all my other courses, I felt like finding a team was like playing dodgeball in gym class. Individuals are chosen and whoever is left over goes to the team with the uneven number. I was always the last to find a partner.

My classmate Leon had chosen me to be his partner. It was even more surprising that I had been chosen to be the lead project engineer. The team was successful in completing the project on time, and we received a B, the highest grade in the course. I was still not satisfied. Again, in college professors have their own grading scale. My senior design professor was not known to give out any A's. My team worked hard to ensure we would earn an A. We exceeded project expectations. Our professor even stated it was one of the best project plans he had ever seen. He found ways to deduct points. I fought with him about the topic. Our team not only deserved the credit, but we earned it. So I pondered how to get the credit that was due to me. Even before any work had been handed out, our professor had the perception that everybody starts out with a B. It's an unfair assessment to be judged by. I put up a good case as to why he should reconsider and give us a higher grade. He stated those were all valid points, but the grade would not change. I looked back to where I had started. In the beginning I was scrambling to get a C to survive engineering. Now I was fighting for an A to thrive in engineering.

The assignment became how to change the perception of our professor. What did he expect from an "A" student? Ultimately I wanted to prove to him we were beyond "B" students. The process began by visiting my professor at his office hours. The discussion centered on his prior experience in consulting for manufacturing facilities. I was seeking to understand his mentality. The key takeaway from our conversation was that he wasn't up to date with the latest trends in manufacturing. Academia had clouded his vision. He had been so far out of touch that he didn't know that old manufacturing methodologies won't work with more technologically advanced products. In speaking with my team members, the discussion was centered on going beyond the textbook. That meant researching the new wave of manufacturing facilities. What are the products, tools, equipment, racking systems, and mechanisms that make the process successful from the time material enters to when it leaves the plant? This is the bread and butter of Industrial Engineering. The idea was to compare the textbook with the professor's lecture. As luck would have it, our IE advisor took the students to a material-handling expo in Cleveland. This is where companies showcase their products. My team member and I decided to split up and visited as many booths as possible. The plan was to collect product brochures and business cards. After going through about 20 or so, we decided upon a couple of different racking systems. We contacted the companies for pictures and cost of equipment to include in our financial report. We were thinking outside of the box and not doing exactly as our professor expected us to do. It was also a risk. The project had taken a different direction.

The risk paid off. We succeeded in changing our professor's perception of grade classification. I completed my final design course with an A. My professor had given the same senior design project out every year. He was impressed with our fresh perspective. He mentioned to us that he as well had learned something new. We'd set the bar high and excelled over it. I was beginning to feel proud of the progress I had made in engineering school.

I may have been moving forward in engineering, but hardly any progress was being made in diversifying the field of future engineers. This bothered me all throughout my collegiate career. I will never forget the feeling of sitting in my freshman Engineering class surrounded by Caucasian males. It was a complete cultural shock. It was like being on a deserted island. In the beginning, I kind of segregated myself. The more I became comfortable in my own skin, the more I integrated into the atmosphere. When we are in situations beyond our control, it takes courage to hang on. During this time I met my good friend Kenneth. Kenneth was an African-American student majoring in Industrial Engineering. It was very rare to see both a female and male black student in the same program at Youngstown State. He faced similar situations as I had, but on a different level. The bond that we formed would give us internal strength to press forward. We wouldn't let each other fail. To keep me encouraged, he asked me, "Why give up now and waste all the miles we have traveled together?" Kenneth graduated a year before I did. I was happy he made it, but lonely looking for encouragement to wrap up my fifth year. I just felt not enough was being done to encourage blacks in STEM. It is one thing to attract minorities to STEM; it is a completely different thing to keep them there. It took a while, but I give the system credit for offering a paid research internship. I had been selected by my academic chair to be in Glen Stokes Research program. I worked with a faculty member and local business to solve a real-world business problem. It was all about engagement and exposure, allowing minority students opportunities to succeed outside the classroom. My professor had given me my own assigned research lab. Participants in the program had a chance to go on field trips. African-American women played a key role at NASA, so I was intrigued by visiting the NASA Glenn Research Center to learn more about space. The program concluded by me giving a poster presentation of my project to peers at Ohio State University. The atmosphere was uplifting. It was the motivation I need to close out my final year in engineering.

I came, I saw, I overcame, and I conquered.

Overcoming obstacles in post-secondary education took more than strong will and determination. There were practical things I had to implement. It required me to think and perform on a different level. The biggest challenge was figuring out how to overcome my learning gap. I could read but couldn't comprehend. I could hear but it all was just noise. I thought tutoring would help. I started going to the Student Success Center and Mathematics Department. I became frustrated because every time, there was a different person teaching me. Even with the help, I was still far from where I should have been. When did it click? It clicked when I decided to hire a private tutor for mathematics. For one thing, I needed consistency. My first tutoring session with Kris was like no other. Before Kris would help us to solve one problem, she began to draw diagrams. These diagrams were of elliptic and parabolic equations used to solve integrals. I questioned why she was starting here. She explained it was because I didn't understand the concepts. She told me, "When you begin to understand how these equations work, you will then be able to solve the problem. The math will become simpler as you break it down." The pictures she drew helped to put things into perspective. Once I began to understand the concepts, she then worked with me on minimizing errors. She pointed out that when I solve problems, I make small mistakes in not using the right units. This is what prevents me from solving the problem. I needed to pay attention to the details of equations. It was simple math, once you break it down into smaller chunks. Kris did me a huge favor by identifying my learning style, how I learn. I spent twelve years in public education "learning" how to memorize. Memorizing facts without understanding concepts leaves you unable to solve tasks based on real-world situations, measurement concepts, and geometry. Once I figured out what caused the learning gap, it was time to find solutions.

OVERCOMING THE SYSTEM: ACADEMICALLY

You have to **define your learning style.** This is the first step. There are four primary learning styles: visual, auditory, read-write, and kinesthetic.

Visual learning is a style in which a learner uses graphs, charts, maps, diagrams. You may be a visual learner if you:

- Are a fast talker

- Exhibit impatience and have a tendency to interrupt

- Use words and phrases that evoke visual images

- Learn by seeing and visualizing

Auditory learning is a style in which a person learns through listening. You may be an auditory learner if you:

- Speak slowly and tend to be a natural listener

- Think in a linear manner. Meaning you think in one sequence after another. After one comes two, and after two three.

- Prefer to have things explained verbally rather than read written information

- Learn by listening and verbalizing

Read-Write learning is a style in which you learn best through words. You may be a read-write learner if you:

- Prefer information to be displayed in writing, such as a list of ideas

- Emphasize text-based input and output. Your mind thinks like a computer. You input/and or select data on the screen and then the program provides you the output.

- Enjoy reading and writing in all forms

Kinesthetic learning is a style in which you learn by doing. You understand how a clock works by putting one together. You may be a kinesthetic learner if you:

- Tend to be a slow talker

- Tend to be slow to make decisions

- Use all your senses to engage in learning

- Learn by doing and solving real-life problems

- Like hands-on approaches to things and learn through trial and error

Defining my learning style was my biggest breakthrough. It helped me to determine how I learn best. It provided me a baseline to measure how well I was performing in the classroom. Not all teachers, educators, and professors teach the same way. The second step is to **Measure** your learning style in each individual classroom. You can use your quizzes and tests as the baseline. Our performance tells us what we know really well. It shows us the learning gaps.

The third step is to **Analyze.** Identify the cause of the problem. Why don't I understand something? The fourth step is to **Improve.** Come up with ways to get better in the areas where you lack understanding. The fifth step is to **Control.** Find what works, develop a plan, and stick with it.

My Achilles heel in college had been Physics. I defined my learning style as visual. They say pictures are worth a thousand words. I measured that my learning style did not best fit with how my teacher taught the course. On the exams I gathered that I struggled to solve equations that required first solving other equations. It is called find the derivative. The professor never gave us the problem straightforwardly. His teaching style was strictly lecture-based. To get a grasp on Physics would require me to adopt other learning styles. I did not fully understand equations to derive them. For example, I knew force was equal to mass times acceleration. I had memorized that.

On the exam, we had to solve for the force. My professor's teaching style didn't change. The change I made to improve was finding an online resource. I wanted to learn the same material, but from a different professor. Academic Earth is a free online course platform. There are courses on every subject matter from the top universities in the country. I began using this platform as a way to better learn physics. I started watching basic physics at Massachusetts Institute of Technology.

I am a visual learner, so I was more in tune with the online courses. For students to understand a concept, a live demonstration was done in class. It helped put things into perspective. I gradually made improvements in physics and no longer felt completely lost. I incorporated academicearth.org into my control study plan. Success begins outside the classroom. It's what we do after the class lecture that makes a difference.

I will be the first to admit that I never adopted good study habits. My study habit was to cram the night before an exam. If I had questions, I was out of time to get them answered. Second, I cheated myself by not taking my education more seriously. I was studying to become an engineer. How do you develop a successful study plan? It will be different based upon how you learn and retain information. The "Guaranteed 4.0" system was developed to give students a blueprint for academic success. The creator of the system guarantees a 4.0 if all steps are followed or she will give you $100. I discovered this resource after college at a conference. It's been proven to work by hundreds of students. This is one tool I encourage you to invest in and use.

So what's an African-American girl to do in an all-white male environment? The answer is to integrate, not isolate. It was uncomfortable in the beginning being the only African American and female in the classroom. The introvert in me wanted to isolate myself. But I knew that would only push me further away from my goal. I thought back on my history. During the Civil Rights movement, there were people who fought for me to be in this position. They struggled so I could have a seat at the table. Sitting at the table wasn't comfortable, but I knew it was necessary. I saw myself opening a door that another African American would enter into Engineering. I came to the conclusion that just because I was the only one did not mean that I didn't belong. My place was in Engineering. It was up to me to find a way to network with my professors and classmates. It took a while, but I figured it out. One day the professor ended class early, saying we would continue at a local pizza bar and restaurant. I wasn't into drinking. It's part of the social aspect of college. My professor saw me and told me I was going the wrong way. I replied that I didn't drink. His response was that he could get a pitcher of iced tea. I thanked him for the offer, but said I was just going to head into work a bit earlier.

In the beginning it never dawned on me that was his way of building relationships with his students. I began to go just for the free pizza and wings, minus the beer. It's where friendships were formed that made all the difference in the classroom. The key is seek to understand, not to be understood. In time, I had become one of the guys. I got invited to study groups. If they had information regarding class exams and quizzes, they would be sure I knew. My male classmates showed confidence in my competence. There were times when they looked to me to help them out with homework assignments. The courses where I struggled, I gained bonus points with my professor for hanging out at that pizza place. It's all about playing the game in college. My only regret was not playing the game sooner. You don't have to do as they do. When the opportunity presents itself, take the chance to integrate socially. I decided to also join the Institute of Industrial Engineers chapter at our school. All positions were filled except for secretary. I elected to become the secretary and keep things in order.

Within each system there are support organizations. The National Society of Black Engineers (NSBE) was founded to increase the number of culturally responsible Black Engineers who excel academically, succeed professionally, and positively impact the community. This is a student-run organization on campuses across the country. There was no NSBE presence on YSU campus when I came. It did not come back into existence until late in my junior year. An African-American Chemistry professor decided to oversee and bring it back to life. Many chapters on campus have 50 to 100 members. Our chapter was very small: we only had five members to start out. For any club or organization to be successful requires full participation and teamwork. We could never grow our organization beyond the five members. We had many ideas, but failed to execute them. Members used classes as an excuse that they were too busy. I argued that the organization needed to be treated like a class for it to grow. I was secretary of the organization, but at times played the role of the president. Our president at the time refused to step up and accept the challenge. I believe it's good to be involved in organizations where you can learn and grow into a leader. I was disappointed NSBE didn't grow as I had hoped. I envied other colleges where NSBE had a strong presence.

NSBE is the best organization by far for black engineers. Every year the organization has its national convention. The first time I went to an NSBE organization, I was stunned by how many African-American engineers were in attendance. NSBE draws more than 10,000 people every year. The conference hosts workshops, career fairs, events, and meetings for attendees. The atmosphere was electrifying. It kept the fire in me burning. I remember at the conclusion of one meeting, we began chanting and singing. So we decided to exit the meeting marching and singing down the hall. It's not every day you get to be in that type of environment. There are many benefits of being a member of this organization, other than inspiration. NSBE provides its members a scholarship database. NSBE job portal allows you to create a resume to share publicly, so employers can find you. This is a place where you can seek out opportunities for internships and jobs. Every year NSBE hosts the conference in a different city. You get to travel and see different sights and sounds beyond where you live. Yes, it requires funding to go. I encourage you to invest time studying their platform. You will be amazed at what you can learn and do.

What if I'd known about NSBE sooner? There is no telling where I would be. This is why I felt compelled to write this book. I want you to be informed about organizations that are dedicated to helping you succeed. You don't have to go it alone. You will have those days when you will want to give up. Others may persuade you to do so. They may try to lead you to easier majors. Ask yourself what it will cost you in the long run. I remember my advisor proposed for me to consider Engineering Technology. At YSU they did not have an Industrial & Systems Engineering Technology degree. I was told it was more hands-on. Students had the option of getting a two-year or four-year degree. It seemed like the easy way out. Employers don't view Engineering degrees and Engineering Technology degrees the same way. An Engineering Technology degree is what a lab assistant is to a chemist. Working now in corporate America, I see the difference. We have many people with Engineering Technology degrees who now assist engineers building samples and gathering test data. They are contract employees who do not receive salary, benefits, or paid vacation. I often considered switching to a Liberal Arts degree. I have met several people with Liberal Arts degree now working in retail. We never really know the path life will take us down. With an Engineering degree, it can lead you on many different routes. The character that you build is invaluable. You are better prepared to face adversity. There will be nothing too hard to overcome because you will have the problem-solving skillset.

The goal always seems impossible until it's done. The world in which we live is calling for more. In order for the United States to remain competitive, we have to diversify the science and engineering enterprise system. This requires more.

More engineers who build better communities.

More engineers to send people on commercial flights to space.

More engineers who discover cures to diseases.

More engineers to design new advanced technologies.

More engineers who write their own history.

There is a blank page waiting for you. Create the future!

Part II

Entering Corporate America

Chapter Three

Preparation for Success

May 15, 2010. There I was sitting in Beeghly Auditorium. I had survived Engineering School. The sleepless nights, tears, and all my failures had paid off. The commencement ceremony didn't seem real. Was this all a dream? It was a dream that became reality. Never would have made it through Engineering School without God and my family. There were many days they sat and listened to me crying. They were my motivation to keep pressing forward. For a class assignment, my niece Bryanna was asked to write about someone she admired. Out of all the people she could have chosen, she wrote her report about me. That was why I was sitting in my commencement ceremony. I wanted my nieces and nephews to see that "impossible" is just a word. I wanted them to visualize themselves sitting in a commencement ceremony.

As the ceremony ran its course, my mind began to think back on the journey. For someone who doubted, second-guessed, and didn't believe in the beginning. Was this my career purpose, to be an engineer? I overcame the many internal battles by the grace of God. Things did change for me once I dedicated my life to Christ. School didn't get any easier, but faith carried me through. I learned not to lean on my own understanding. I sought wisdom from a higher being than myself. I was amazed the road God brought me through to get to that point.

I wondered where God was taking me next. I would graduate from Youngstown State University without a job offer. I had applied for hundreds of engineering jobs online, but received not one phone call. I failed to impress employers at the NSBE convention in Toronto. The first night in Toronto, my fellow engineering students and I had been targeted. Our rental SUV was broken into. While in a restaurant, one of my bags was stolen, which contained my passport, resumes, and cell phone.

I spent the rest of the evening at the Toronto police station. The next morning I had to go directly to the U.S. embassy. There I was given a letter to enter back into the

U.S. After this crisis was handled, we made our way to the NSBE convention. Without my resumes, I had to put together something from scratch. I entered the NSBE and just began to talk to any company. I was unprepared as some recruiters asked me, "Well, tell me what you know about our company?" At NSBE they had interview booths and many companies hired right onsite. I was given the opportunity to interview with a couple of companies. Nothing came of it. I asked myself, "How do I stand out in the crowd?"

I walked across the stage at graduation wondering what the future held for me. College was behind me. The real world awaited me. Out in the world I was jobless. With a degree in hand, what was the next step? I needed a job that would hold me over until I got into the engineering position that best suited my interests.

My professional work career started at a financial services company. The company creates data and software for investment professionals. Software provides financial data and analytics for investors to make decisions. I was hired in September of 2010 as a Research Analyst Intern. It was not my dream job, but for $10 an hour it was a start. I felt this was better than flipping burgers at McDonalds. The size of the company was small, only thirty employees in the Youngstown office. The employees were divided into two teams, North America and International. I found myself on the international team. The culture in this company was very diverse. There were interns from India, Russia, China, Pakistan, Saudi Arabia, and of course the United States.

Our job was to profile international companies in different sectors. This required thorough research, reading companies' annual reports. The annual report is the company's yearly report to shareholders, documenting its activities and finances in the previous financial year. Bottom line is learning where and how companies make their money.

The job was a great start to my professional career. But after a few months, I started to feel unfulfilled. For five years I had worked too hard to just settle for anything. In this job I excelled, but I felt like anybody could. They could have paid a high school student to do what I was doing. The daily tasks became boring to the point where I didn't feel challenged anymore. How did I get here? Why was this the first road traveled after college?

I chose not to intern while in college. One reason was I didn't own a car, so it would have been difficult to get to work. Second, I favored the convenience of working on campus instead. A decision that I would soon regret. I should have found a way. An internship would have made me more appealing to companies: 90 percent of companies are looking to hire candidates straight out of college. The catch is companies like to see that you have some experience. The more you know coming in, the less you will have to be taught onboarding into a company. My advice is to begin looking for internship opportunities in your field. I recommend as early as sophomore year in college and no later than junior year. An internship will help to build your resume. You gain experience beyond the classroom. Textbooks will only teach you so much. Having an internship within your field shows you firsthand what the career is all about. In our minds we envision a career being a certain way. The real-world experience may show and tell us things we couldn't have imagined. It will help you figure out whether this is the best career for you.

Am I ever going to make it into a real engineering job? This is what I asked myself daily as I sat in front of the computer researching companies. I was gaining valuable knowledge. As the saying goes, knowledge is power! It only becomes powerful when you know how to use and apply it. I had used knowledge gained as my beginning point to take the next step. It's a job looking for a job. The key is to be strategic with a plan for job hunting. Industrial Engineering was my background. So as an aspiring industrial engineer, I had to first decide what I wanted to do. If you don't know where you want to go, any road will take you there. Seeking our life's purpose often requires us to look within. The answers are not always there immediately. It's a process. The process began for me by doing the following:

Step 1: Establish Career Goal

My career goal as an industrial engineer was to become a continuous improvement specialist. The objective was to identify and improve the outcomes of manufacturing and operational processes to improve efficiencies, reduce cost, and increase customer satisfaction. Ultimately I wanted to climb the corporate ladder. Reading stories about women such as Ursula Burns was inspiring. Ursula Burns was the first African-American woman to become CEO of Xerox. It was proof to me that the glass ceiling could be broken. We are capable to lead.

Step 2: Determine Industry

Determining what industry to establish my engineering career took some time to figure out. Research was required to see what industry had the highest demand for engineers. Where were manufacturing facilities located? I was going to have to leave Youngstown, Ohio. Manufacturing jobs in Youngstown are a thing of the past. The aerospace, food manufacturing, and healthcare industries were my target industries to seek out employment. Why these three industries? I thought it would be an honor to work on projects that helped the many men and women protect our country. The Food Network was my favorite channel to watch on TV. I love to watch how factories make the foods we buy and eat at the grocery store. Food recalls are huge, as they have led to many illnesses and lots of money lost in manufacturing. As a continuous improvement specialist, I envisioned myself playing a key role in this industry. As an industrial engineer, I care about the wellbeing of others. Working in the healthcare industry was another option, improving the layout and flow to ensure patient needs are being met in a timely manner.

Step 3: Build Your Brand

Resume

Your resume is what sells you to an employer. It's a story that describes who you are, what you do, and how you can bring value through your skillset. Your experience plays a factor in whether a company views you as a potential fit. I had failed to gain real-world experience. My backup plan was to use my senior design and research projects to showcase my abilities. More importantly, the key was having the right professional look. There are a million different ways to write a resume. A Google search brings up many examples. It is also good to have examples as reference, but those should not be copied. Create a resume that's uniquely you. I am no expert in this area. In creating my professional marketing tools, I consulted with my college career services. We worked together collectively to build a resume that presented my strongest abilities. People have a tendency to overstate or embellish on their strongest abilities. While I believe in not selling yourself short, I don't believe in lying about who you are. It can very well come back to haunt you. Be true to who you are and the right opportunities will present themselves.

Social Media Platforms

Resumes are not the only way recruiters screen candidates. How we live our lives through social media plays a major role. Platforms like Snapchat, Instagram, and Facebook are all about interaction. Interact with caution. Ask yourself, What would an employer think if they saw pictures of me half dressed? It is attention seeking in all the wrong ways. Would you show up to work dressed provocatively? Image is everything. Keep a professional-looking profile. There are videos that go viral. The popular one seems to be people fighting. Fight club videos are not good to have on any of your pages. It is unwise to take video footage of people arguing or fighting. This can be seen as encouraging conflict. I played it safe in this area by keeping my interaction on these platforms limited. The one social media account I recommend leveraging more is LinkedIn. LinkedIn is a career-building tool. Top things to consider when building a professional career page:

a. Professionally taken photograph

Your image speaks volumes about who you are. It's your first impression to viewers. **DO** get a professional headshot picture taken. **DON'T** upload a selfie.

b. Create a unique headline

Determine your brand moniker. Every job comes with a title. There are many others who have the same title. A headline that reads "Industrial Engineer" most likely won't stand out from other industrial engineer profiles. Just like a breaking news story, your title should grab the viewers' attention and compel them to read your profile. On my profile page, I had the title of Project Coordinator. I did a search on LinkedIn and saw so many other project coordinator profiles. This resulted in very few page views. In updating my profile, I changed the headline to Change Agent. It does make one stop and think, What does she do? Since making this change, the number of page views had gone up.

c. Write a summary about YOU

This section should POP with personality. One should not just copy what is on a resume. Use this section to tell viewers who you are and not just what you do. You don't have to write a book on yourself. I would recommend no more than three to five sentences for this.

d. Describe work experience

In describing your job experience, don't just write what you do. Recruiters like to see the value you bring with results. Begin by putting together a technical portfolio. This can be a PowerPoint presentation that highlights your projects. I would advise not to include confidential information that the company has stated should remain private. Here is an example:

I was the lead project coordinator for a digital

harness build board. The digital harness build board purpose was to increase an individual's time it takes to build a product. In describing this experience, the highlight is to show how I increased operators' build efficiency by 30 percent. My technical portfolio would show any cost savings that saved the company money by implementing a new technology. LinkedIn also allows you to upload videos, where you could feature a short segment of your project.

It's important to help people understand the value in what you do, how you do it, and how it could help their organization.

e. Connect with a strong network

It's not a matter of what you know, it's who you know. I would encourage you not only to connect with those in your immediate circle but look to connect with like-minded people you can learn and grow from. If there is a particular industry of interest, seek out the industry experts. You can study what makes them successful in that industry. Leverage what you learn through your connections to build upon your professional career. Also there are companies and special interest groups that you can follow.

f. Think It. Write It. Post It.

LinkedIn has a tool where you can share your thoughts on any subject. I believe in the power of voice and establishing your brand message. What topics are you passionate about related to your career goals? What have you learned that can be shared with those in your community? Sharing your thoughts in a blog gives readers an inside look at your thought process. Recruiters may view it as you defining more of your role in the corporate work space. Companies will hire you for what you know that brings experience. Becoming a thought leader is one whose message can be influential.

Don't worry about doing it "right" all at once. Your professional profile will change as you evolve and become more familiar with the online platforms. Develop a plan to build your professional career profile. Strategize how you will showcase your abilities. Assess how your professional profile is doing based upon page views, who's viewed your profile, and if it leads to opportunities.

Step 4: Sharpen Interview Skills

Every interview process is different. There is no way to predict what you will be required to do. Get comfortable talking about you and your experience. Many people get nervous during this process. Based upon your resume, your interviewer will learn your background history. It is up to you to provide details. Pitch yourself to the employer. Understand from your work experience what you have done, actions you have taken to complete the job, what tools have helped you succeed, mistakes made, lessons learned from mistakes, and how you work with people. Recruiters are trying to see how well you may fit in. Sharpening my interview skills was best done doing mock interviews. A mock interview is a simulation of an actual job interview. It provides you with an opportunity to practice for an interview and receive feedback. Check your career counseling department on campus to see if they provide this type of service. Constructive criticism is good if it helps you get better. During my mock interviews, I learned I spoke too fast. The feedback was for me to speak more slowly. This would allow the opportunity for the recruiter to understand and follow what I was saying. I didn't realize I said "umm" really often as a filler word. My goal was communicating a different way and choose my wording really carefully.

Interviews can be conducted in all types of settings. One interview setting is over lunch. I attended etiquette training as another method to sharpen my interview skills. It was a basic crash course in table manners in a professional setting. Make an investment in books that provide best strategies to interview. One book I heavily relied on was *250 Job Interview Questions You'll Most Likely Be Asked,* by Peter Veruki. I considered it my roadmap to navigating the interview process. I made index cards with interview questions. I would read the question out loud and practice how I would answer. With preparation it gave me confidence knowing I could go far in the job interview process.

Step 5: Proactive Job Hunting

A lion hunts its prey. Job seeking is no different. It is time consuming, and it can be a full-time job. Strategize how you will market and position yourself to land interviews. The recruiting process is evolving. Understand the industry trends and how companies recruit. Many organizations host virtual career guidance webinars. Formalize a strategy. I implemented various techniques such as applying for jobs online, working with headhunters, attending job fairs, and utilizing my network. If your professional network is limited, turn to family and friends. I told my family my career plan. My sister's neighbor worked for Ohio Edison. She asked him if he knew whether they were hiring engineers. He gave her information on who I could call to ask about job hiring. My friend's mother was the Human Resource Director at our local hospital. He asked her if the hospital was looking to hire engineers to help with efficiency and improve layout. I spoke with her myself a few times about opportunities. There were no openings at the time, but I knew all this information gathering would one day pay off.

Through it all remain patient, as the hiring process can be very slow in many companies. Do not become discouraged if your application is rejected. I've heard more NO's than Yeses. Every no moved me one step closer to a yes. I grew personally and professionally throughout the job-hunting process. The people I got to meet and the places I got to travel to were worth it. Through it all do not doubt yourself when it does not work out. See it as God having something greater in store for you in HIS divine timing.

Chapter Four

Finding My Place in Corporate America

O n June 20, 2011, my engineering career began at an automotive company. I was hired as an advanced development process engineer. My engineering group was responsible for developing advanced technologies for factory automation. The primary goal was to reduce manufacturing costs through eliminating manual labor. The company had just come out of bankruptcy. I was part of the first group that the company had hired in ten years. I was overjoyed because I had finally arrived. When you start anything new, there are so many unknowns. I had to learn not only my own position but about the company as a whole. A new workplace required me to build new relationships, learn the company lingo, and understand how they run the business.

As part of my career development, I was paired with a mentor. He had been with the company for almost 30 years. I would be his understudy. I would learn what he did in his role in preparation for if/when he retired. Automotive had an older workforce of Baby Boomers. The biggest drawback I saw in the culture the first few days was the age gap. The group of new hires were all in their twenties, and the experienced employees primarily in their late fifties. I was working with co-workers who had children the same age as me. The company felt the need to hire new individuals who could retain the knowledge base. But I could not relate to my co-workers. I was just beginning to make a living, while they had been doing it for a long time.

In the beginning, there was a feeling of uneasiness in the facility. Many viewed the new hires as a threat. They felt their job security was in jeopardy. Some people were under the impression they would be forced out of their position because the company was starting to hire new people. This sparked a level of competitiveness, everyone looking out for themselves. My mentor and I worked well together. My first few months he put together a plan just for me to learn what we do. He introduced me to key people within the organization whom I would need to network with in the beginning. He felt I didn't need to be introduced to every employee because it would be hard to remember them all. After each introduction he recommended I create a who's who list, writing down people and their job functions. One basic but powerful tool was that he required I begin to use a work journal/log to document the details of all my projects. I learned very quickly that people suffered from amnesia. It was important to track projects, changes, and any issues so there would be a record of it. My mentor shared with me his experience and what he had learned over the years. He was very open to telling me the history of how things came to be. He taught me the basic fundamentals of our company's product. He laid the foundation for me to grow in knowledge and have a better understanding. Whenever I had any questions or doubts, he would answer them. We were like peanut butter and jelly. We were always together.

Just as there are pros to mentorship, there are also cons. He and I had a few disagreements. Our company had a global ADP process meeting. This meeting required engineers from each region to present their projects to the global executive committee. My boss wanted us to present more projects to showcase our group. I had not been assigned a project. Everything I was working was in conjunction with what my mentor was involved in. My boss and mentor wanted me to present a project, but I was afraid of looking incompetent. It became a debate. I could sense my mentor was getting mad, as his nostrils were flaring. He told me because he had more experience, I had to do what I was told. There was a pattern: when he felt threatened that he was losing the argument, he always threw his experience in my face. But just because I had little experience, that shouldn't mean my opinion didn't count. He wasn't the only one to pull this card; there were other co-workers who did it as well. I wondered whether they could see the value I brought. If everybody thought alike, then nobody was thinking at all.

There were times when I would propose an idea of how to execute a project and I'd say that it didn't make sense to do it. Our hybrid prototype shop floor was growing in business. The floor had very limited space. The team needed to define a plan to reorganize and remove excess material, tools, and cabinets to open the floor. My recommendation was to consolidate cabinets and tools that had all the same things. Once the consolidation was complete, cabinets would be marked to be removed. This seemed like a good first step, because it would take longer to remove excess material. The lab needed to identify which material was still needed for jobs. I presented this to my mentor and the team. Nobody agreed to move forward with the plan. Three weeks later, my mentor presented the same idea, but when he said it, things began to take place. During our conversation, I stated this had been MY idea. He acknowledged that but gave no explanation why he didn't buy into the idea when I had stated it. If I had a good idea, he would say he just couldn't envision that working. The team was on a condensed timeline to incorporate a new wire harness build board. The accessories for the board were very expensive. Our company has their own manufacturing lab. I recommended we utilize 3D printing capabilities. The idea was turned down. Two weeks later, my mentor wanted to look into getting the accessories 3D-printed. The supervisor of the lab wanted to implement the idea when he proposed it. I had spoken to this same supervisor earlier about the idea.

I was starting to see the culture for what it really was. My ideas were not embraced on many occasions. I had learned this was a culture where men's egos stood in the way of women being heard. I questioned why I'd been hired. I wondered if the company was really ready to embrace change. It crossed my mind that they only hired me to fill their diversity gap. I was the token black woman. The culture made me feel like I should just be happy to be there, regardless of whether I was contributing. My purpose in engineering was not to be my mentor's assistant. I wanted to remove myself from his shadow. I felt like I had no identity. People had come to know me as the girl working with him. When I was out and about around the facility, people would ask me where he was. When I would do an assignment, I would be asked whether he had reviewed it. It was frustrating that my co-workers did not trust me. My boss asked me to put together some labor estimates for a robotic machine. I reviewed it with him, explaining the details of how I used the global labor standards. He seemed satisfied with it. It turns out he wasn't. Behind my back, he asked my mentor to do the same thing and then used that estimate instead. Not a good way to empower somebody by discrediting their work!

Over the course of months, my relationship with my mentor began to change. He spent less time guiding me along the way. I was left to make my own way. It was hard to do when the leadership from our boss provided no clear vision for the team. The culture's leadership direction was like the weather. It changed daily. It made it harder for me to try to position myself to be a subject matter expert. There were people who were heavily relied on for their knowledge. I aspired to be known for something. There were guys who were innovators in their positions. They had patents and trade secrets from the company. I had nothing to show for my work. All my projects led to a dead end.

There were times I wished I had a female mentor to look to for advice. The sisterhood of women in the culture was missing. There were 330 employees in the building, only 50 to 60 of them female engineers. The culture was so male-dominant that the decision was made to take away one of the women's restrooms. They converted it into another men's restroom. Then my boss introduced me to another woman, saying that she would serve as my mentor. She openly admitted she did not know a thing about mentorship. I learned quickly that the few women in engineering were not interested in helping me advance my career. They were more interested in knowing all my business and every detail of my personal life. When I had lunch with the female mentor, the focus of conversation was always about who I was dating. The conversation would also be about office gossip. My mother had taught me that if they gossip to you, they will gossip about you. I didn't trust confiding in her about my life. When I needed support in a situation I was facing, very little was offered. I knew I could not turn to her for career advice. Beyond grade school, I didn't think women acted petty. The dress code in the facility was business casual. But I found there was a change in attitude the days I wore my Sunday best. I noticed hardly anyone would speak to me because I was dressed better than they were. As women, I felt we should have been more united. There was a need for strong bonds to have a support system, but we were divided.

While it's good to have people you can lean on for advice, I have learned that nobody can lead you to the career path destined for you. As I tried to make my own way, my boss felt the need to micromanage my every move. I understood I was still in the early stages of my career. But the micromanaging and his personality made him come off as an insensitive bully who liked to throw his "superior" status around. He had no real knowledge or vision of what it took to lead a group responsible for innovation. Instead he used bullying tactics to make up for his lack of competence. Sitting in his office, he made it a point to tell me he was the boss. Here was yet another person trying to level up on me and throw their title in my face. For what? He didn't want me in the corner alone working on my projects. Part of his micromanaging plan meant I had to schedule a weekly meeting to review everything. I was assigned to work on a machine vision project to inspect wire harness accessories. This required me to look for vendors to partner with. I sent out some general inquiries on the project requests. My boss wanted me to forward all the emails I sent so he could read them. In our review meetings, he criticized me for moving too slowly. My plan was too methodical. He stated we needed to deliver. During this particular project one of the suppliers I was working with passed away. I informed my boss of this. His response was heartless. What bothered me the most was that he tried to make a joke about it in front of others. I can't find humor in somebody's death. To keep up with his demands, I found another supplier who could implement this project for us. I did all this work for the project to go nowhere. The project got canceled because management didn't want to put their money where their mouth was.

The company tagline was "innovation for the real world." Innovation required us to take risks and make bold decisions. But it was all just talk. The culture was still living off the past, scared to turn over a new leaf. A lot of the indecisiveness affected our group directly. Everyone on my team was constantly spinning our wheels. Everything we worked on would lead down a dead end. I felt I was given all the impossible projects. Enough to keep me busy, but not enough to be incorporated in a manufacturing facility. Doing some research, I discovered the light guide system. This technology transformed manual assembly operations. It served as an assembly aid. The projector system would show images on the work surface table. The operator had visual aids to show them the build sequence of how to put a product together. My boss liked this concept and wanted to incorporate. I did all the work in establishing the relationship with the company. I was extremely excited to work on this project. My boss then decided to assign it to another individual.

My boss moved me around to other areas, but they were all lateral moves. These other areas presented challenges. I was put in a position to work directly in the lab to help do the methods engineering for a lot of the programs. Going into this position, I knew nothing. It required me to learn from someone else. The culture and mentality didn't lend itself to teaching. The individual who was given this notice became very defensive and aggressive. She didn't view it as a collaboration, but indeed that her job was being taken away. I could see her point of view. I just didn't know how this company was going to move forward if the people were holding back. We eventually overcame the job security obstacle. She began to teach me new things, to understand how wiring drawings were supposed to be done. In return, I helped her organize and coordinate the workflow by introducing a program tracking system.

This lateral move was short-lived and I was moved to another area. This time I would be taking over for a contract engineer. He served as the foreman for the electric vehicle charge coupler line. The company wasn't completely eliminating his job. He was going to work part-time, two days per week. This was my boss's plan, but he had no direction how to execute it. This was all learning on the go. The guy I was working with had no organization for how he did things. He didn't even follow the print half the time. It was hard in a sense because I was trying to figure out how to learn the job the "right" way. This was my first project where I worked directly with operators who were building the parts. There were so many factors to juggle. The line was supported by electrical and mechanical engineers who built the stations and machines. My first big test came when the general foreman went to Italy for a month. It was hard to lead when the people you were responsible for knew more than you. How could I tell them anything when I was just learning? Running this line was so chaotic and there was also a material issue or machine down. This is where the shop floor supervisor decided to micromanage me. This line was a part of his lab and included in his budget. He provided the people to build at the line. I noticed when the general foreman was there, he wanted no part of it. When I became in charge, he wanted to be all involved. I knew more about what was going on than he did. I would give direction on one thing and he would override me. He would tell the operators something else. He would want to give direction until the point it was time for us to build something for management. He would then flip the script and say it was all me. I hated this position because I felt there were too many cooks in the kitchen. I personally stopped talking with the shop floor supervisor. Many of us got the impression he was insecure. My presence bothered him.

The charge coupler line taught me so many things. For manufacturing to be successful, we needed continuity. The operators were always changing. The customer started to raise questions about quality. The general foreman agreed we needed to have the "A" team and not the minor league team. Due to the operator turnover, we needed a system of training to incorporate new builders into the process. The foreman didn't have any training documents. I created documents to include at every station in the line. Engineering support for when machines were down was a hassle to deal with. Many of these guys worked in functional areas that required them to work out of town. I saw the need for a preventative maintenance plan on what to do when systems fail. I thought trying to get this line organized with all the resources was hard.

My hardest assignment was dealing with an operator who came to work after being beaten up. This woman's eyes were black, her mouth was busted, and she looked completely in pain. I wanted to get on her for not showing up to work the day before. She never called in, but now I understood why. I was lost as to what to do or say. I laid my hands on her and began to pray for her healing. I said if she needed me to do anything, to just let me know. It was hard to see someone suffering. I didn't care how many parts she produced that day. I wanted her to get better physically. The crazy part about the situation was we had a huge customer visit from one of our major customers to see the line. I wouldn't let her stand out there in shame. As the tour passed, I took her through an alternate route of the building to avoid the crowd. What people go through personally could affect them professionally. I quickly found out how the culture handled these situations. There was no official protocol on how to deal with employees who may have suffered some type of abuse. The managers talked about the incident, but turned the other way. Did they turn away because they didn't want to interfere with employees' personal affairs? Or was management just not trained to handle sensitive situations?

They never explained why, but I got pulled away from the line. Once I learned the process, it was not challenging. It was a babysitting job. My potential was not being maximized. I went back to working on impossible projects. Even being a woman of faith, it was hard to be grateful in any and every circumstance. The passion started to fade. I could see I was on the fast track to nowhere. I believe I was suffering from a career identity crisis. I felt I wasn't known for anything compared to my male colleagues. Many of them had patents and trade secrets in their name. They were sought out for advice and insight. I would wander aimlessly searching for my place within automotive. It crossed my mind to begin looking for another job. What experience had I gained thus far? Nothing that was beneficial for a resume booster. My frustrations were made known on my personal business plan, or PBP. PBP's are for employees to set goals based off company objectives. Establishing goals is hard when there is no clear path.

I spoke up to my boss, who answered by throwing me in a fire. The biggest assignment in my career was leading a team to develop a plan to implement a robotic bending cell in our manufacturing plant in Juarez, Mexico. The Ohio process development team transferred programs all the time. We would teach the Mexican workforce about the product, implement equipment in the plant, and perform process handoff duties. This robotic bending cell was different. It would be the first robot installed in a plant. There was pressure from executives that every product line had to have a flawless launch. There are so many details that have to be covered to execute a flawless launch, basically making sure the supplier fulfilled all customer expectations and requirements on time. The biggest launch metric was having no major disruptions or issues that would cause the production plant not to ship product.

Being new to the program management role, I had no idea what formal procedures existed. My confidence was a bit shaken. How could I lead if I didn't know what I was leading? I questioned whether I had the leadership qualities to lead a team of men. There were many challenges I was up against. The biggest challenge of all was communicating through language barriers. My first encounter when trying to speak with a

Mexican engineer turned out to be a game of Pictionary. He couldn't speak English very well, and I don't speak Spanish. It was awkward communicating without saying a word. We used PowerPoint as a communication tool describing the process with pictures, arrows, and text on the screen. This interaction occurred in a face-to-face meeting. I wondered how I was going to effectively run meetings online. The first few attempts failed miserably. My mentor and I were the two industrial engineers on the project. Our role was to define how to build the wires through each assembly station. There were two wires that needed to be built. Each wire was identified by a black or red stripe. They were two different lengths in millimeters. Both wires needed to be passed through an aluminum tube that the robot would bend into shape. My mentor and I didn't see the value of assembling the wires individually. Both wires would be built together throughout the assembly process.

That was the first communication failure. Not all team members were on the same page. The Mexico team couldn't comprehend what I was trying to describe. I tried describing the method through a process flow diagram. My follow-up to the process flow diagram was pictures and videos. No matter what tool or method I tried to use, my message was unclear to the team. The Ohio team understood the process, but I got no backup support on the phone from them. They would sit on the conference call and just let me struggle through it. I would soon learn that members on the Ohio team were not onboard with the idea. This led to a huge argument between two senior engineers. My mentor is a smart guy. He offered good advice from his years of experience. I had noticed at times he wanted people to agree with him so he could be right. He got into a heated debate with the process engineer responsible for building a solder station for the project. I am not one for drama or conflict. It was uncomfortable to watch one man talk down to another man. As the project lead, I felt it was my responsibility to provide a solution, but I didn't know how. When the senior process engineer explained his side, I could see why he was hesitant for us to build two wires at a time. Ultimately it wasn't our decision to make. The Mexico team would need to provide their input on what they felt was best to do. The company did not provide any translators. My boss had joined a few of the conference calls I ran. He told me I needed to change the way I spoke. I will admit I am fast talker. He thought if I spoke more slowly and changed my vocabulary, it would help. I accepted that as constructive criticism.

I also changed communication tools. Progress was

made as the Mexico team began to understand the process of how to build the product. From their standpoint they didn't want to build two wires at a time. They felt it was a high risk that could lead to high scrap in having to throw a whole assembly away. My next challenge was to deal with meeting participation. As the weeks went on, there was no representation from the Mexico team. It was understood that their main focus was on "current production" (what the plant is building today and dealing with all the issues). The program I was leading was future production (what will be launched in the plant in the coming months). Why should they be concerned about something that has yet to happen? The goal was to eliminate all issues and address questions on both ends to avoid any startup delays. The cultural difference is what divided us. When companies started sending jobs to Mexico, American engineers lost all the power. The mentality of the Mexico team was that they had been building wire harnesses for twenty-five-plus years; they didn't need our input. It's only when a problem occurred that they looked for our help, but it was more to point the blame in our direction. Knowing this information, I still had to find a way to bring all team members together. I found it difficult to hold those accountable who wouldn't show up. I had asked that team members send a representative if they couldn't attend meetings; they didn't. I sent email communications asking for status reports; I never got any responses.

I was the program leader, but couldn't get any involvement. This job assignment taught me that management will put people in positions of authority, but not give them any power to make decisions to get people to do their job. My boss continued to use the cultural difference as an excuse. I couldn't hold the Mexico team accountable, but I would hold my boss accountable. If I failed, that meant he failed. In our group meetings, I began to call him out. It wasn't to embarrass him, but to challenge him in his role as a manager to move this project forward. He had spent much time flexing and telling me how he was the boss. I put it out there that he needed to act like the boss and resolve these high-level issues. In helping him resolve the issues, I provided evidence that the Mexico team was a no-show. During meetings, I would track attendance of participants. I stated to my boss all the issues we were up against if we didn't get full participation. The message was spread to the Mexico team managers. Participation increased in my meetings, but it began to die down again.

I was stressed beyond measure. There was so

much to control in this project. I had to not only focus on the production end but to manage every aspect. I felt burdened, but who could I turn to for support? I had to heavily rely on my faith. I prayed to God, How could I lead a team that didn't want to be led? How could I lead a team where members of the team were having mental breakdowns? I turned to God for direction. The verse I meditated on daily was Proverbs 3:6: "In all your ways acknowledge him and he shall direct your path." Prayer and meditation helped me get through this project. I couldn't control what other people did. I could control what I did. I held myself accountable for all my actions. I had to set the tone and lead by example. The assignment didn't get any easier, but I got stronger as time went on. What bothered me most was all the changes being made. I couldn't get the design release engineer to freeze the drawing. It made it difficult to plan for a production launch. Our customer wanted to change the connector on the wire harness. The company wanted to implement a new Tyco terminal and connector. They wanted the connector implemented on the harnesses that were due. I explained to my boss all the things this change could affect.

My boss, wanting to people-please, agreed to make the change. The major issue was the connector was not yet released. I had spoken to procurement about purchasing the material. In response we got a huge lead time and large minimum quantity order. I immediately went back to the design release engineer. The release engineer sat at our customer center. I challenged him on his change. I stated if he wanted it implemented, he would have to help get the material. After all the hoops the team jumped through, he had the nerve to change his mind again. This is where I put my foot down. I explained the change had already been implemented, there was no going back. My teammates applauded me for standing firm on my decision.

Production programs are in jeopardy 80 percent of the time because of material availability. From a process development standpoint, we could react to changes on the fly. Our material suppliers could not. One was due to constant changes from the customer. Second, they needed to ensure they had raw material available to produce the parts. The lead time for wire cable was sixteen weeks. Typically with material, you could substitute for another part. This would require a work order change on the print. This cable situation had everybody pulling out their hair. There was no substitute for this cable. We could only purchase it from one supplier. Procurement was able to get me a partial order delivered in a reduced time frame. Business can be shady. Your goal can be sabotaged because another individual wants to play the hero. The Mexican procurement team was preparing for this program. They had begun to order material. They were unsuccessful in acquiring all parts. They had turned to the Ohio team to help supply material. We couldn't supply material because we were building with it. The Ohio procurement coordinator and I explained this to all parties. The Mexico team went behind our back and spoke with the Director of Hybrid Engineering. He knew the situation we were in. To boost his own ego and play the hero, he agreed to give Mexico our material. I was in shock. There was nothing I could do about it. To make matters worse, another person decided to go behind my back and use the cable for their program. I had fewer components and no cable. This was a huge red flag that could have potentially shut down our customer.

As the program leader, I raised the issue. I left it up to management to decide if they wanted to solve the problem. Meanwhile I continued to work to bridge the problems closer to solutions. The real test came when we had to train the Mexican process engineers to run the robot. As an alternative to the automatic robot, a manual bender was developed. It was Plan B in case the robot failed in production. Plan B was rejected by them.

The Mexico team was all in agreement for the automatic robot. Management insisted we ship the manual bender as a backup. So much time was devoted to training the Mexico team. During that time I was able to build relationships with them. It was difficult to collaborate in phone conferences, but I used the face-to-face interaction as a way to work better together in the present and future. In order to move the project forward, I needed to first learn and understand how they thought. I wanted to learn their way of implementing new processes. My methods counterpart taught me how to communicate and document issues. The production plant used a formal open issues tracker Excel file. This was better than just stating all the problems in email format. It made a huge difference. Management and team members were more responsive. There were some differences of opinion on how to build the product through the cell. My counterpart and I went back and forth several times. I tried to bring us to a common ground. I let him win the argument not because he was right, but he would take on the process. I knew if the issue was raised with management it would become political. Things would not work in favor of the Ohio team.

The Ohio team spent well over four weeks, working with the team in Mexico out of Plant 5. It seemed all our efforts had gone to waste. Plant 5 was over capacity. It was stated they didn't have the floor space for the robot and its equipment. Our executives made the decision to move our customer's product business to Guadalupe, Mexico. Our customers didn't like their product being built in the interior of Mexico. During a conference call, our executives stated they would have the conversation with the customer about the business transfer. Guadalupe III plant sent a new team to Ohio to be trained on the robot and equipment cell. With a new team came a different set of expectations. I was learning every step of the way what it took to start up a line on the production floor. So much of the Mexico team time was invested in the production floor. I had come to understand why they didn't call in to meetings. At the same time, I expressed how important it was for them to know what was coming to the production plant. Problems could be minimized on the production floor if advance preparation was taken into account.

This project pulled me in all types of directions. While managing the project, I was supposed to be doing the methods work involved. It all got away from me as I had to help manage the high-level problems. I was supposed to design a wire insertion station. This station would be a table that held the aluminum tube. Wires would be inserted and slid through the tube. There were so many details that got looked over. When the Mexico team came for training, they brought up a lot of things I did not consider. Resources for the project were limited. Many of the team members were doing three times the normal workload. Then came the additional support in helping resolve issues. Being in a leadership role, I had to learn how to pull back. There was one instance in particular where the Mexico application engineer wanted me to help her solve issues related to the product drawing. During our conversation, I stated she needed to resolve print issues with the design release engineer. It was difficult for her to get his input. There were way bigger problems that needed to be resolved. I just couldn't focus all my time and attention on every single matter. I did offer her recommendations as to what she could do next. If I did all the work for her, then what would she be left to do? No matter how hard the assignment was, we all had to work through the roadblocks. I had to empower people to step up and take responsibility.

The final stretch of this project was shipping it all to Guadalupe III plant. This was the biggest task. During this whole project, I had come to learn more about the company and its systems. You don't necessarily know the way until it's time for you to go in that direction. The day came when the robot and the manufacturing cell left Ohio. I felt a huge weight lifted off my shoulders. It was a mission accomplished. I was in the public library unwinding my mind in a book. Then I received a phone call that changed everything. My boss called me to check the status of the robot. I explained to him that the robot had shipped. Our customer was not in agreement with the business placement. Our executives had failed to persuade them. The truck was well beyond the border. There was no turning back. I spent the night talking to the dock supervisor about next steps. The next morning was full of chaos. We had to coordinate how to get the shipment from Laredo, Texas, to El Paso, Texas. I was just amazed by the lack of good decision making on the part of our executives. They were a factor in the equation of stress. Doing the paperwork for the original shipment was frustrating, now to coordinate the move was just a complete mess and nightmare. As always, the team found a way to pull through. When the chaos settled, the Ohio development process team executed a flawless launch.

I arose from the very fire they thought would burn me. Who could expect me to succeed? Nobody. I turned some heads during this project. Some of my co-workers commended me for doing a good job, despite what I went up against. A few had my back and spoke to my boss about all I had to endure. Many began to see my worth and what

I brought to the table. My boss admitted in the beginning he was worried. He credited me for getting better as the project went on. The last night the Mexico team was in town, we ended up having a team dinner. After dinner my boss handed me an envelope. He was awarding me a certificate of Excellence for Outstanding Coordination and Leadership. And I got an additional $500.00 in my paycheck. It was my boss's decision to have someone mentor me. At my performance review, he admitted my mentor was the one holding me back. I told my boss that although I had a ways to go, I felt I could stand on my own two feet. I had received an Outstanding job performance rating. He said it was the first he had ever given out. The company would be handing out bonuses, and mine would be higher than expected. I had finally seen the fruits of my labor.

It took some time, but I felt I had arrived. When projects needed to be strategically planned and executed, I was the one called upon. As the lead Project Manager for advanced development, I was the one who took conception of a product and made it into a reality to manufacture. The journey requires endurance. I stumbled along the way, only to get back up. I failed along the way, but have grown wiser learning from mistakes. I doubted myself along the way, but have yet to give up. There have been days I felt weak, but I found that inner strength to keep going. I questioned whether I belonged. Now I stand in confidence, no longer questioning because I know I belong. There is a place for me. I am making room for you. Stay with me on this journey. Together we will succeed.

Chapter Five

Stay the Path:
Career Lessons & Advice

T he number 10 is a significant number for women in STEM. The majority of women in engineering leave the field after 10 years or sooner. The main reasons are the workplace environment, with its gender bias, discrimination, and lack of representation and career advancement opportunities. In doing research, I've come to learn these reasons are not tied only to the STEM fields. Barriers black women face exist everywhere in corporate America. The Lean in Foundation conducted a Women in the Workplace study that found that 54 percent of African-American women report often being the only black person in the room at work. 23 percent of African-American women feel excluded, and 41 percent feel under pressure to perform.

The Lean in Foundation study brought to light a couple of things. One, our society and the world we live in have MORE work to do in embracing diversity. Two, no matter what the black woman aspires to be in life and where she decides to work, there will be barriers. Jackie O'Hara, a molecular and cell biology scientist said "Women in STEM matter because women matter; diversity in STEM matters because all people matter."

You must stay the path. Staying the path matters because you will become a part of history. In previous chapters of this book, I highlighted the accomplishments black women have made in engineering. We come from a heritage of rich accomplishments. We must build on our history. You will be a history maker! In 2018, I left the automotive company to join a paint company. I was the first African-American woman to ever work in a powder coating facility for this company. It's not the number of years you work, it's the quality of years. I worked at the paint company a year and seven months. During that time I implemented work standards for training and development of our workforce. Mistakes were minimized as employees became more knowledgeable about the process. I led a study that uncovered a major flaw within our system. We were the first plant to implement new industry combustible dust standards. I became the subject matter expert for other plants to consult with. I opened the door for our company to hire an African-American process engineer. She became the first African-American process engineer at the Charlotte plant.

History tells the legacy of those from the past. We will not know who tells our story, but we must leave a story to be told. If you stay the path, one day someone will tell your story and the contributions you made to engineering. A historian once told me that if you want to live forever, then you must build for eternity.

I'm in the ninth year of my engineering career. It has crossed my mind several times to leave engineering when I reach ten years. Statistics and trends can lend themselves to changing the course of people's direction. We follow trends and what seems to be popular in our culture. During high school, there was a fight after school between two popular individuals who were beefing. Everybody was going to see this drama unfold. When I got home I told my mother about the fight. My mother's advice was to never go toward trouble; go the other way. I told her everyone went toward the direction of the fight. She followed up and said, "You are not everyone. I'm not raising a follower. Never follow the crowd, even if that means you have walk home alone." I lost count of how many times I had to walk home alone and miss all the after-school fights. My mother's advice is something I used all throughout my life. I asked myself why I wanted to leave engineering after ten years. One of the reasons was because all the other women had left. I was no longer with some of the women who had started in engineering with me. I'm not a follower. I am trailblazer.

By leaving engineering, I would become part of the problem. I would then be counted as part of the statistic of the number of women who left. As we grow in life, our aspirations and ambitions change. People want to do something different with their lives. My passion for engineering runs deep. There is nothing else I want to do but be an engineer. I choose to be part of the solution, to stand in the gap and advocate for women in STEM.

The fight for women's equality has been a battle. We will not win it all in a day, month, year, or decade. As women fighting for change, we will make progress that makes the workplace a little better for those up-and-coming engineers. It will then be your responsibility to drive change forward for those coming behind you.

Staying the path is just not about diversity. We need

more women in STEM roles to make scientific innovations useful and safe. Technological innovations will not be relevant if we do not take into consideration the needs of half the population. The Huffington Post provided a good example around this point in an article stating that when seat belts were first invented, they were modeled solely on the physical attributes of men. When it was first introduced as a safety measure in cars, several women and children died because their physicality had not been considered.

More recently it has been discovered that there are male inventors behind the development of next-gen menstrual products. A popular fitness tracker company came under fire for setting its period tracker at 10 days. It is believed that on average a woman's period lasts no longer than a week. If this company would have consulted with more women or had female engineers leading the project, it would have been discovered it is not the case. There is a population of women who suffer from PCOS (polycystic ovarian syndrome). These women have longer periods or have no period at all. These are things men don't know when they are brainstorming in the boardroom on how to develop a product.

Without diversity in STEM, technological innovations

can only go so far. STEM is the enterprise system that makes the world go round. Without women a part of this system, we will not make progress in advancing humanity forward. Staying the path ensures we are doing our part to make the world a better place.

You have come to learn reasons why there are so few women in STEM. Politics and bureaucracy are the common denominator among them all. No matter where you go, these obstacles will be there. This is what has caught women off guard in the field. Awareness and lack of experience of not having to deal with it in their K-12 education and college plays a role. STEM programs are designed to be hands-on, engaging, and interactive. Within these programs, young women learn engineering skills. These programs do not provide insight on the harsh realities of working in Corporate America.

You may enter the workplace thinking you are well prepared because of your degree. Textbook knowledge is all theory. It provides you a foundation. The world is your teacher and there is a lesson in everything. You only learn lessons through experiences. Through my experience and learning from others, here are career lessons I've learned.

Career Lesson #1: Own Your Destiny

Don't think of yourself as an employee, but instead an enterprise. Me, Myself, & I, Inc. YOU must define your OWN fulfillment and success. No single path for success exists. There is no corporate ladder. Sheryl Sandberg, COO of Facebook, said "careers are a jungle gym, not a ladder."

The State of Black Women in the Workplace study revealed that 29 percent of black women are less likely than men, white women, Latinas, or Asian-American women to say their manager advocates for new opportunities for them. Engineering is a competitive field. Corporations hire the best and brightest talent. Your manager has gained a very valuable asset that will help take the company to the next level. A commander will not give up his best general and watch someone else win the war. Neither will your manager. By losing you to a promotion, their value goes down. Politics behind why a manager may not advocate for new opportunities for you is because it has the potential to decrease their budget. They will not be able to replace you with another resource. This will set the manager and the team back in fulfilling expectations. I've experienced the opposite of this. There were managers who came to my boss inquiring about new opportunities for me. My boss never told me. I eventually learned this from others as they came to me and wondered why I hadn't followed up with them.

Do not leave your career in the hands of others. Never assume hard work is what gets people promoted. I believed in this philosophy in the early stages of my career, and it got me nowhere. No man on earth can define your life's destiny. The career success you seek must come from within. The road to destiny is paved through history. Study your history, as it will be the blueprint to show you where to go.

Own your destiny and find opportunities to promote yourself. One of my female colleagues excelled at this. She didn't wait to get noticed. She was proactive and made bold moves to advance to the next level. Her career journey taught me that success does not come from a place of comfort. She took on an international assignment that expanded her skillset and network. When she returned from Germany, she came back better than when she left. Due to her growth, she was promoted to supervisor. We started together in 2011, but our careers were no longer in sync. She leveled up because she owned her career. Be in the driver's seat of your career, not just a passenger.

Understand that career promotions are a marathon

and not a sprint. There will be instances where some people seem like they are on the fast track. This is often due to having a little luck, timing, and the state of the business. Don't compare someone else's career journey to your own. Each of us is unique. Success has many different meanings. Define what success means to you.

Career Lesson #2: Find a Mentor

A manager may not advocate opportunities for you, but a mentor/and or sponsor will. It's important that you build your network. Show me your network and I will tell you how far you will go in your career. At times you will struggle. This has nothing to do with how intelligent or capable you are, but reflects a lack of knowledge of how to navigate through different work situations. Learning from someone older, wiser, and more experienced is an invaluable business opportunity. Within your network you may find such an individual. Finding a mentor is a process that could take time, as you learn who individuals are in the company. I was fortunate that I didn't have to find them; they were assigned to me. There were many ups and downs, as in any relationship, but I'm grateful as I look back on those moments. Here are some ways to identify a good mentor:

- They are great at what they do

- Outstanding role model

- Strong people developer

- Motivational & Inspirational

- Able to address mentee's needs and goals

- Excellent communicator, able to draw people out, listen, and share

- Trustworthy

- Committed

Another alternative is to ask the company about their mentorship program. Many organizations have resource groups specifically for African Americans. Within these employee resource groups, the committee will pair you with a mentor. Don't feel entitled that a mentor owes you his/her time. You may feel obligated that they should reach out to you. They are not in need of guidance, you are. Commit to making time to speak with your mentor and come prepared. As they learn about your career goals and aspirations, they can introduce you to people within the organization, as well as provide guidance on opportunities you should explore. In automotive there was a manager who offered to be my mentor. I had first met him at NSBE. He was there recruiting on behalf of the company. In my seven years working at automotive company, we've spoken twice: once when I started with the company and again when I left. I regret not taking advantage of that opportunity. What I experienced in automotive company could have been different. He was an African-American male who had learned to play the game and navigate the jungle gym. All I had to do was reach out. Learn from this lesson and don't make this mistake.

I've learned that mentorship can be informal. Pay attention to the conversations you have with people. Within the dialogue they are giving you free game. Don't overlook people just because they don't appear as a mentor. When I started working for an HVAC company, my manager told me to work with a senior staff engineer. Together we had to lead the organization in switching to a new time-tracking software. In working with him, I came to learn he had mental health issues. Why take advice from a guy with mental health issues? Well, he taught me more than my manager did. Things I didn't know existed or I needed access to, he showed me. This helped tremendously in reducing my learning curve. Not what I expected from a white male colleague with health issues. You will have allies in the workplace to help you succeed. Only 26 percent of black women agree that they have strong allies. You must not focus on who is against you, but who is for you.

While you may admire mentors, role models, and colleagues, do not get caught up in walking in someone else's shadow. Learn from them but remember to embrace your own greatness and BE YOU!

Career Lesson #3: Learn & Grow Everyday

A person never appreciates something until they don't have it. If you switch companies throughout your career, you may find there are no mentors or mentorship programs. A mentor is not an excuse for you not to learn and do your own job well. Nobody is going to hold your hand and babysit you all the time. Expect to learn the job on your own. You have to make it your responsibility, investing in your **S**kills, **A**bilities, and **K**nowledge. As an enterprise, you own the rights to your potential. The greatest return on investment is the realization of your own potential.

The job does not come with a manual. Management will not draw the blueprint for you. Pick up the pencil and draw the blueprint. When I became the first African-American process engineer, I had to create the blueprint.

In figuring things out on my own, I was lost! Faith isn't faith until it's all you are holding on to. I was born with problem-solving abilities. How to train and develop myself was the problem to be solved. In the development of self, one must become a self-starter. Learning how to do the job requires motivation. Use motivation to pursue further education without the help of others. Being a self-starter has always been part of who I am.

There was a job description, but that's all. To familiarize myself with the process, my boss did have me work in R&D and quality, and shadow his production workers. Everyone in production did the job differently. (One operator told me he would just push buttons until the machine did what he wanted it to do!) Training and development was lacking on all levels. Learning the basics, like how the powder coating process worked, helped a bit. The critical and most technical details of the job were left unknown. Being the first plant engineer, I wanted to set the bar high. How do you reach that level of success with no baseline? Every expert was once a beginner. How do beginners begin?

Step 1: Learn the System

In my manufacturing system, powder was the output. Know what you are manufacturing. Determine the inputs to the system. Defining the system will require you to spend time in the area the product or service is being manufactured. Shop floor and production floor will become your teacher. $Y=f(x)$. Y equals outputs. X equals inputs. A systematic approach to learning the job is utilizing the DMAIC process. The acronym is **D**efine, **M**easure, **A**nalyze, **I**mprove, and **C**ontrol. This process comes from Lean Six Sigma methodology. Within each phase there are tools that can be utilized to teach, identify, train, and solve problems. Use the Define phase to learn the operating system. Follow the process that leads to the product (output). Use a notepad to create a process flow diagram. Get to know the employees. People will recognize that you express a vested interest. They will open up to you. You will learn the process, but they will also point out the problems. Value stream mapping is a powerful tool. You are still creating the process flow, but time is added to each sequence. Value stream map provides you an overall idea how long each step in the process takes. Document the bigger picture.

Secondly, begin to learn the technical specifications if dealing with pieces of equipment and machinery. Utilize manuals to understand the theory behind the equipment. Create a document matrix. List each piece of equipment, write how it functions, and add any technical specifications. This will become your road map in trouble shooting. You will have an understanding of what the process/system was designed to do vs. what is being monitored. Following this methodology helped me to look at the process from a different perspective. Everyone was focused on the powder coating. If we continue to focus solely on the output, we miss opportunities to better ourselves.

In doing research I discovered the system was pneumatic conveying. Pneumatic conveying is a material handling system that uses compressed gas to transfer bulk materials such as powders through a pipeline. I had discovered the "what." The bigger picture became known. The next step was "how" pneumatic conveying operated. At that moment the learning curve grew steeper. Doubt had set in. The manufacturing system was like Goliath. It was huge. I had no knowledge how to go about solving the issues.

When in doubt, Google. My counterpart at our Grand Haven facility gave me some books. One of the books was a pneumatic conveying design guide. PBE became my go-to website. PBE was the center of expertise on all things relating to my industry. Creating that resource catalog was beneficial. PBE offered free webinars by industry consultants. Webinars may not give you the answers you need. They are beneficial in learning the basics, hearing the presenter's perspective. Ask the "stupid" question. Leverage the consultant's knowledge. It's free advice. Webinar material helped me to think through how it applied to my situation.

It's critical to be in the know. You will come to learn who the key players are in the industry you work. Never become complacent in any job assignment. Grow within your role. Attend technical conferences that are relevant to your job function. You may find it challenging due to cost constraints. Showcase the value and how the company will benefit from it. This still may not work. I took it upon myself to invest in conferences out of my own pocket. All I did was request permission to have the days off. If it's within your control, remove the obstacles.

Grow in confidence. Nurture your career by growing every day. Growing in your job may require you to go back to school. Many organizations have employee scholars programs. The company will cover 80 to 100 percent of tuition costs. Also a lot of companies allow their employee to dedicate a couple of hours a week to study and complete coursework. Before taking advantage of a program like this, read the fine print. Be intentional by setting professional development goals. Learn one new thing a day. Keep it simple. It does not have to be anything hard or complex. Learning and growing on the job is about building up your intellect. Learn a little bit each day. You will drown yourself trying to swallow the ocean in a day. Learning can be a challenge. Don't wish for fewer challenges, pray for more wisdom. Uplift yourself with positive affirmations. **YOU CAN, YOU WILL, AND IT WILL ALL WORK OUT**. Keep a journal of what you have learned each day.

LinkedIn learning is a great tool as well to learn a lot of new skills. Utilize LinkedIn to build a network with mentors and consultants in your field. Try to engage in a dialogue with them. Look for things they have done in the field. Use the information as an ice breaker. There are a million ways you can approach learning the job. Always remember you must create the road map. Own your career and navigate it.

Career Lesson #4: Know Your Value

Have you ever heard the saying that your worth should not be tied to your bank account? Whoever came up with this didn't want to pay women fairly in the workplace. Women are underpaid in their profession.

We struggle in knowing our value and how to negotiate in terms of our yearly salary. We sell ourselves short, by leaving money on the table. This hurts career earning potential. Speaking from personal experience, I left money on the table. I didn't negotiate my first job offer. After countless job interviews that led to many rejections, I was just happy to have an offer. Anything was better than the $10 per hour I was making at the time. Based off your skillset and the job market, you must know your value and evaluate it.

Once you get your foot in the door, opportunities will come your way. When you build experience, the world begins to open up with more career options to consider. Know your value. The job market does not play fair and they will lowball you if you let them. A headhunter told me to set career financial goals of where I wanted to be five, ten, and fifteen years from now. Once you set the goal, work to get to that level. Working in automotive, I was underpaid from what was expected from me. My salary was not competitive with what the market said I should be earning at my level. Be strategic in getting maximum value for your efforts.

To increase your earning potential, you may have to leave your company. This was the case when I moved from Ohio to Indiana to start a new job. Evaluating the job offer was much harder due to relocation. Take the emotion out of proposing your counteroffer. A career coach told me the baseline for countering a job offer is a 15 percent salary increase. Now other key factors that have to be considered are: job market, cost of living expenses, healthcare expenses, and relocation expenses if not covered by the company.

Don't be afraid to ask for more. My paint company's offer was low. It's not what you wish for, it is what you ask for. After doing the research and having data to back up my offer, paint company agreed to increase my base salary from their initial offer. Negotiating is a skill. How you use the skill will be different depending on the scenario. Chris Voss, former FBI hostage negotiator states, *"Life is a series of negotiations you should be prepared for."* From his book *Never Split the Difference*, I learned some key strategies to better position myself in salary hike discussions.

Through interviewing and negotiation, I've learned to secure the bag, but not chase the bag. Don't chase money! I had the opportunity of a lifetime to work for a billionaire at an aerospace company, working on projects that enable humanity to live and work in space. There is always a price to pay for living out your dreams. Accepting this position would have required me to move 2,244 miles across the country. The offer was enticing and even included shares in the company. After researching cost of living, taxes, and various factors, I decided the offer was not sufficient. This aerospace company was private, so I couldn't research how much the company was worth to understand whether the stock options were worth it. Human Resources would not provide this information. A counteroffer was submitted and they went up a little bit. The Human Resource manager told me it was the best they could do. In negotiations, I've learned not to be completely fixated on the number. I strategically approached this discussion with the value I would bring to the company.

The aerospace company had primarily been doing research and development and were making the transition into manufacturing. I had previous years of manufacturing experience. In fact, in my interview they knew nothing I talked about because they hadn't experienced it. I'd given all sorts of ideas to consider. My interviewer took notes on my recommendations and at times asked me to re-explain some concepts. They told me you're going to bring a lot to this company. I declined their offer. As a woman of faith, I believe there was no need to chase money. Taking the offer would only move me farther away from my family. The starting base salary didn't measure up to the economy. How far your salary stretches is directly proportional to the region of the country you live in.

Having trust in God, I knew in HIS timing, he would open the right door for me. Proverbs 16:9 says commit to the Lord, and your plans will succeed. Several months later, I'd receive a call from another aerospace company. They offered me the position to become a manager. In previous salary negotiations, I'd utilized payscale.com and salary.com. Considering this job role, the Bureau of Labor Statistics was part of my analysis. The offer was more than what the other aerospace Company offered me. In learning from my previous mistakes, I negotiated for more. Rapper 50 Cent once said know your value and then add tax. One follow up call was all it took for them to agree to my salary counteroffer. I remained steadfast in my faith, and God blessed me. I was relieved I didn't have to move across the country for a higher salary. My work commute was reduced from fifty minutes to fifteen minutes. Successful negotiations are based on give and take. I got the salary I wanted, but my manager wanted me to start the job right away. I got hired in mid-December. I wanted to start my new job in January so I could enjoy Christmas, but I agreed to start work the week of Christmas.

In knowing your worth, you must also stand up for yourself. As a woman of value, you are to be respected regardless of your skin color, gender, and beliefs. Never allow someone to belittle you and never accept any type of harassment. You will be tested, so choose how you address issues wisely. More importantly, protect your peace and your energy.

Career Lesson #5: Understand the Bottom Line

Business is never personal, it's just business. The state of the economy causes companies to shift directions to handle financial hardships. On August 30, 2017, we received the shocking news that the Vice President of our division had decided to shut the hybrid development lab. This lab built all the low-volume harnesses for automotive original equipment manufacturers. My supervisor called us together to break the news.

The lab shutdown would affect forty contract technicians. Nothing happens overnight. Management had known for months. Looking back on all the events that occurred in the previous months, it all made sense. People's livelihoods were at stake. I felt terrible about the state of the lab. We couldn't talk with technicians about it.

I was informed that the lab cutting operator had another job offer. I debated whether I should tell him about the situation. I did. He explained he wasn't sure if he would accept the position. It would be a longer commute. I told him about the situation and said his supervisor would give him details.

Two days later the shop floor supervisor broke the news. The cutting operator thanked me for the insider information. I was just trying to live up to the people caring value. Our management was certainly not. The hybrid lab had been the unsung hero in many circumstances. The lack of quality in our Mexican plants was a constant problem. There were times technicians from Ohio would go troubleshoot and fix harnesses. Who would prevent a major crisis from occurring now? Our customers loved visiting the facility. They could see how their product was being built. Changes could be easily incorporated into the drawings. Customers preferred not to travel to Mexico. Employees discussed how customers would take this news. The heart and soul of the product was the people who built it. So much was sacrificed to meet demanding schedules. Technicians would work around the clock. On some days I would arrive at work as many were just leaving to go home. They would be back within a couple of hours. They were making sacrifices to put the company in a position to be successful. Who would fight for these employees?

Companies will do what is in their best interest financially. Automotive was in good standing. *Business Insider* said we were the "darlings of Wall Street." One questioned what made the company so profitable. It was at the expense of the employees. Management defined it as cost cutting. Nothing but greed. Management got their bonuses. Shareholders got return on their investment. The business does not make money by itself. It takes people to work the business and generate its profit. Bottom line is the money, not the people. Bottom line is you will lose colleagues along the way.

In May 2017 I witnessed a whole engineering department get eliminated. Although I was not among them, this was hard for me. For many this was déjà vu. Black Tuesday was when engineers received an email notice that it was their last day with the company. Within an hour they were expected to gather their belongings and leave for good. Pensions were taken away from the individuals who did not get let go. Certain individuals were knocked down in pay. The company filed for bankruptcy, which is why these types of moves were made. A financially stable company was beginning to go through this vicious cycle. In late 2017, all employees were put on temporary layoff. Now being permanently laid off was the biggest issue. Through it all, I remained safe. I questioned for how long. Many signs indicated that the ship was sinking. Seeing many things unfold taught me some lessons. There are lessons within lessons. Understanding the bottom line, here is what I've come to learn.

Sacrifice may gain you nothing.

I learned this lesson through the stories of senior engineers. My mentor was an overly dedicated employee. In the early part of his career, he traveled all the time to vehicle assembly plants. This level of commitment required him to be away from his three small children. His son would be crying as he walked out the door. One senior engineer said to me he wished he had spent more time with his children. Every testimony was different, but they all said they wished they had done things differently. All they had given was taken away. They had worked all those years to build up their life savings for retirement, and then it was gone. I was advised not to get caught up in making work my life. My former college dean gave me this advice: we work to live, not live to work.

There is no security blanket.

There is no such thing as job security. Companies are loyal to the board and its investors. Everybody is expendable. Don't work in fear of being fired someday. Job security is one thing you will not be able to control. You can only control how you respond. I recommend having a Plan B that takes into account how you will pay for living expenses. It's important to set up and fund an emergency savings account for rainy days. If you lost your job, what would be your next step? You would probably look for another job. The advice given to me was never put all my eggs in one basket. Don't depend on one source of income. Create ways for you to have multiple streams of income. Reflect on your passions and hobbies. Could you find a way to monetize those?

Keep a professional portfolio.

You started your career and are comfortable in your position. As time goes by, you have invested thirty years into the company. One day the company decides to let you go. What to do then? Where would you begin to look for another job? At that stage, your skillset may be outdated. Keep your resume up to date and current. As you gain new skills, add them on. Times have changed. Nobody stays with one company their whole career.

Know how the job market is changing to see what skills are in demand. Grow, evolve, and incorporate changes in your career to make yourself relevant and valuable. Even if you're not looking or need to find a job, stay open-minded when opportunities present themselves. Keep your network strong with headhunters and job-recruiting firms. I see so many of the senior engineers who are struggling to move on. They have been in their comfort zone for so long. It has caused them to lose sight of the world outside the company.

In understanding the bottom line, you must smell the cheese often to see if it's getting moldy. When companies decide to downsize, it may be an indication that it's time for you to move on. Pay attention to the signs, be led by your own intuition. My colleagues said I was crazy for leaving automotive company. I was tired of working with a dark cloud hanging over me. This dark cloud was becoming a burden. Every day my job was in question. Multiple times, I had to put presentations together on my assignments and the value they brought to the company. There were rumors that our group would be the next to get eliminated.

I wanted to leave automotive company on my own terms. After seven years, I felt it was time for a fresh start.

My former colleague texted me after I left and said my former boss and colleagues' jobs had all been eliminated. He told me I made the right decision. I stayed the path but just pivoted in a new direction.

Be Aware

Information sharing is a huge part of the company culture. What you share can make or break your career. Be aware of whistleblowers and informants. Keep your friends close and your enemies closer. In a corporate environment, it's hard to distinguish between the two. DISCERNMENT is needed. You will need to be able to figure out which people you can confide in. Ask yourself what you have to gain by telling that individual a piece of information. There is always someone listening and watching. No piece of information falls on deaf ears. People are assigned to be the eyes and ears for the corner office. An individual's job title will never be snitch or informant. You will learn a lot if you talk less, be watchful, and listen more. I learned this lesson through my colleague at my first corporate job. Financial services was a small company with no more than thirty employees. The culture was very close-knit, like a family. We shared ideas, we had potlucks of different ethnic foods, and we would gather for drinks after work. People felt comfortable communicating and being open.

My colleague made a comment about my supervisor. She felt that he was a complete idiot. She mentioned how he would disappear for hours. This was all said in conversation to another colleague. We would soon learn this was a mistake. Someone repeated this to the supervisor. The informant appeared to be a friend who cared, but her true colors were revealed. What did she have to gain by repeating that information? Was it worth it to break that trust? She may not have liked what my colleague said about the supervisor, but that didn't give her the right to repeat it. We were all contract employees trying to get permanent full-time jobs with benefits. Could her competitiveness have been why? I wondered how my supervisor perceived the information given to him. My colleague was a top performer in her industry sector. I didn't want that to be held against her for voicing her personal opinion.

My name was given to the corner office executive at automotive company. Apparently I had violated the clean desk policy. Our engineering director's philosophy was all about appearance. He implemented a rule that banned employees from having cardboard boxes. We received parts in cardboard boxes. We shipped in cardboard boxes. The facility had no real storage area for engineers to keep parts. The only solution was to keep them stored under our desks. I had come into work one morning receiving notice of a violation. I had one tiny cardboard box on my desk. The individual who sent my name in was someone I thought was a friend. We talked daily about life, career, and fitness. This individual was the beautification person. Her job was to plan, manage, and execute facility upgrades.

She also kept the corner office up to date on what people were doing. I couldn't fault her for doing the job. I was in violation. There were far more individuals who violated the clean desk policy. The cubicle next to me was a complete mess. They had boxes, wires, and paper all over the place. None of those guys made the violators' list. I took it personally because I felt she could have talked to me about it. I felt it was petty. What is the motive to submit only a few names, but not all? Needless to say, I stopped talking to her. When she asked why, I told her I had a lot on my plate and no room for chatter.

You will be watched. Someone informed my boss that I was leaving at 3:30 every day. My boss asked me about my working hours. I explained to him that I was working from 7:00am until 3:30pm. I was putting in my time. The only reason I started so early was because of my mentor, who arrived in the office at 6am. I felt it was best to get in early to utilize my time to work with him. My manager informed me I was working outside my core office hours. On my first day of work, there had been no mention of this. The direction was for me to begin my workday between 8:00 and 8:30am and leave at 4:30pm. One day my boss came looking for me at 7:15am. He asked me why I was late. He had told me to come in at 8am. I realized who told my boss I was leaving early. Before I left each day, I would stop by the front desk and chat with the clerk briefly. I began parking in a different location and exiting through a different door.

Focus on the work and not the haters. Do not work in a state of paranoia for fear of being watched. Nine months into my manager position, I received two MVP awards. The Most Valuable Player award is given to high-performing employees within the company. When you do the job well, those watching will see the impact you bring. If they are going to watch, might as well give them a show.

Within the area there were manufacturing plants. Not all employees know each other. At one of our central machine shops, I met an engineer who was friends with a corner office executive. Conversation was small, but he began to ask questions about how I liked it. I gave him the diplomatic answer. It wasn't the opportunity to open up about how the executive director was causing morale to go down. This was a wise decision. He had revealed to me how he had become good friends with the man in charge of running the building.

People will test or bait you to see what they can pull out of you. My company had a rigid structure of governance. Every new product development goes through a phase of governance. Engineers dreaded the process. They didn't understand it. Also it was time-consuming. In talking with a guy, he started getting into how stupid the process was. Nobody pays attention during the gate reviews and the whole system needed to change. He asked me what I thought. I replied that I was there to help teams navigate through phases. He kept asking me, don't you think it's stupid? He questioned what I didn't like about it. I could see what he was trying to do, but I wasn't going to take the bait. In a professional manner, I told him that no system is perfect. Where there are gaps, we could address those in an improvement workshop. You do not know who is connected within Corporate America. Remember to keep this in mind as you navigate your career. Use good judgment in deciding whom to trust. Loose lips sink ships!

Our ancestors made many paths. We cannot let their hard work be in vain. A new generation must answer the call. Find your path and stay the path. Engineer with the end in mind, focus on the deliverables, and work to solve, not manage, the problems.

Part III.

Developing the Engineer Within

Chapter 6

Mindset: Get Your Mind Right

E very life shift begins with a mind shift. How one views life can be from two different mindsets. There is the *growth* mindset. According to American psychologist Carol Dweck, with a growth mindset people believe that their most basic abilities can be developed through dedication and hard work. Brains and talent are just the starting point. This view creates a love of learning and resilience that is essential for great accomplishments." Next there is the *fixed* mindset. Carol Dweck states "people believe their intelligence and talent are simply fixed traits. No time is spent developing them. Their mindset leads them to believe their talent alone creates success, without effort."

To succeed in STEM will require you always to operate from a growth mindset. You can't rest on your laurels. The technical degree will only be enough to get you through the door. Working in the paint industry, I had to get into a growth mindset. The environment was a chemical processing of paint. During the time I was deciding on what engineering discipline to pursue, chemical engineering was at the bottom of the list. I really didn't know where it could take me, and the coursework seemed harder. Funny how life comes full circle. Transporting powder paint through pipes seems easy in theory. It is very difficult, due to all the variables. As stated, jobs can be a challenge when your voice goes unheard. I looked at my role from both mindsets.

My fixed mindset led me to believe I'd reached my full potential. Even with training, there was no way I could do this job. My perspective was based on my past history. I didn't do well in chemistry. Manufacturing was all about chemistry. The plant operated as if they didn't have an engineer. I admitted to myself, I wasn't good enough yet. With any new career transition, there are going to be growing pains. How does one grow through the pain? By going through with a growth mindset. I was limited due to my lack of knowledge.

I made a plan to learn one concept a day about powder coatings, each day building onto the next. Here are some practical ways to develop a growth mindset:

1. Analyze your weakness. Write down what you do not know. In powder coatings, it's all about the system. I knew nothing about ventilation. All pipes and ductwork looked the same.

2. Write down what you need to learn. This can be tricky to figure out. I wrote down that I needed to learn what makes a ventilation system good or bad.

3. Begin research and consult experts. A consultant provided me information on ductwork.

4. Study and practice. It's one thing to learn, but completely different to implement what you learn. I learned T-shaped ductwork is a big design flaw. I picked one section of the plant and began to look for T-shaped ductwork. Understanding the system design helped me to begin to analyze the operating problems.

A growth mindset will enhance your skill, abilities, and knowledge. Negativity exists all around us. It can even live within us. The battle lies within the mind. Keeping it real is a struggle at times. We have to operate in the right mindset.

Society can be brutal at times. I've witnessed firsthand what Corporate America can do to an individual. Guard your mind! The Bible has been the best resource for my success. I am not here to convert you, only to share my own experiences as a testimony of faith. Romans 12:2: "Do not conform to the pattern of this world, but be transformed by the renewing of your mind." This world will tell you that you are not enough. Good enough. Smart enough. Pretty enough. Why should you let their opinion matter?

I reflect on Romans 12:2 often. It's easy to fall into the trap of what the world thinks of us. Constructive criticism is good, but when it is a deliberate attack to tear down, I will not stand for it. I believe God gave me and you talent. A talent that must be refined and improved upon. Don't let what you have not yet mastered destroy you. Renew your mind through positive affirmation. Reading the Bible is my positive affirmation. Find what works for you. It should strengthen, guide, and motivate you. More important, your resource should help you stay in the right frame of mind.

I was so excited to come up with a low-cost invention for the plant. The operators praised me for my brilliance. Behind closed doors, management didn't like it. It was revealed to me what was said. I refused to go down that spiral path, where you begin to question, Am I good enough? Yes, I am good enough. I didn't focus on the negative. The end user of my invention gave me credit. The solution made their job easier. My mindset was focused on things within my control. I no longer stressed out about things outside of my control. Too many times I had fallen in that trap.

Fretting on your job performance evaluation can break your spirit. We all want to feel our employer values us. Teamwork is the game until it's time to hand out bonuses and raises. The system is rigged. I have challenged and fought back. The situation was bigger than me and my manager. Things like this can drive you nuts! I've seen it happen to two engineers while working at automotive company. I didn't want that to be my fate. The serenity prayer helped me to release the weight off my shoulders.

My organization made a huge investment in Oracle. There were a lot of politics behind the decision to move to this software. Migration was one more burden the plant couldn't bear. Every emotion possible came from within the plant: complaining, grumbling, and resistance to change. Operations was required to assign process data for 1300 formulas. It was concerning, because there was no time to do the data the right way. The plant not having an efficient method to collect and analyze data caught up with us. Process data going into Oracle would be inaccurate. Bad data entered in meant bad data coming out.

We had a system problem. The plant was old school, didn't want to change at all. My growth mindset told me to embrace the opportunity. I was dropping the dead weight to free my mind. My team and I had to wing the data. In doing this I put together a plan of attack. The plan would help us when the system went live. The process parameter data would get questioned. I had the methodology on why the data was being shown. Not everybody took my approach. During our cultural transformation workshop, Oracle was the topic of discussion. It completely derailed the objective of the meeting. It had the group stressed. Our corporate reps made a point to put this discussion to rest. Oracle was a huge boulder, a massive rock. It couldn't be moved. The team could move the rocks around it. This analogy eased the anxiety in the room. The key to staying in the right mindset is to focus on what you can control.

Faith kept me going. There is no way we can do it all in our own strength. When it felt beyond me mentally, prayer was my answer: "God grant me the serenity to accept the things I cannot change, the courage to change the things I can, and the wisdom to know the difference." This helps to put the things in the mind into perspective. It provided clarity. Separating the controllable vs. uncontrollable. Imagine going from a team of eight engineers to being THE engineer. Being the only engineer brought a lot of expectation, anxiety, and stressful moments. I loved manufacturing for all the opportunities. Opportunities can turn into burdens. No way could I do it alone.

Management would often ask what our needs were. Every plant had one engineer. The need was the same for all. Engineers felt we needed to develop a team inside each plant. Instead of hiring people, they would send support. The plant "support" system was not working. Every day there was a battle for priorities. Getting pulled in all directions stretched us beyond our capabilities. The state of the business would not lend itself to hiring more people. I began exploring my job options. The environment around you is key to keeping your mind right.

Consider the workspace you occupy daily. A cluttered

desk could lend itself to a cluttered mind. Multitasking is necessary, but too much can lead to a mind just racing. It can cloud judgment on determining the urgent from the unimportant tasks. Speaking from experience, this has occurred many times looking at dozens of piles of papers. Restructuring my workplace environment allowed me to focus. At the end of each business day, I would leave out a sticky note of one to two tasks with a corresponding pile. After progress was made, I would file away the piles and begin again. Establishing an intentional habit of a non-cluttered workspace helped my mind stay at ease.

The engineering profession is all about staying sharp. A mentally taxed mind can derail your skillset. Stress can affect overall performance. Invest time in a hobby or activity. This will enable you to have a positive stress releaser. Do something to help take your mind off work. Many people take their jobs home with them. There is no escape. The brain can become captive to the job. My escape is the gym. Working out four times per week helps me to keep my mind sharp. Many work out for the benefit of a healthy body. I do it for the mental. I burn off that frustration. I lift myself up from the disappointments of the day. I run with the mindset to continue the journey.

I witnessed one of my co-workers have a mental

breakdown. The job became too much for him. He was a very talented mechanical engineer. He became very tired of spinning his wheels. He left our work group and went to work in another department. This did not solve the problem, as he had hoped. He ended up taking some time off. When he returned he seemed better, but still fragile. Pressure to perform often causes one to overthink. It will send you over the edge.

Protect your mind at all costs. Get your mind right! A lost mind can't lead, innovate, or build. Condition your mind to grow. Have the courage to fight the battle within. Focus on what is within your control, set up your workspace to keep you inspired. Work to stay sharp!

Chapter 7

Overcoming Barriers Through D.R.I.V.E.

During a conversation with a historian, he asked me, How have you gotten to where you are today? I've committed myself to the process. Each step of the way there were barriers. Overcoming the barriers came from D.R.I.V.E. within. Many will search the whole world on how to become successful. Who better to guide you than self? The world can provide the answers, but you still have to do the work. Your blueprint and plan will get tested. D.R.I.V.E. will enable you to pass the test, overcome barriers, and break through to success.

My D.R.I.V.E. has been defined by *determination, resilience, integrity, vision,* and *excellence.* Throughout my life I have refused to be defeated without trying harder. The force behind my fight was being determined, standing firm in my intention to achieve my goals to the end. The majority of highway interstates are straight. Picture yourself driving down the interstate. With the exception of vehicles entering the interstate, it's a pretty smooth ride. Headed to your destination, you begin to see orange signs. These signs symbolize that construction is under way. Highway construction can lead to many things. One is that the number of lanes are reduced. This increases travel time.

Barricades are put in place to block off ramps. Detour signs are posted that take you on a different route. You can no longer go at normal speed limit within a construction zone. Construction causes people to panic. If they can't continue straight, they become lost. It frustrates people because the timing to their destination is unpredictable. Barricades cause fear because people can't see a way around them. Such is the case on our path to achieving our dreams. The goals may seem unattainable because of what lies ahead.

Success is not linear. It will not be straightforward. Even with a plan mapped out, expect construction. The construction phase is where people lose heart. The roadblocks may seem stronger than your willpower. Determination is required to see it through to the end.

Batman is one of my favorite superhero movies. There is a scene when a young Bruce Wayne falls down a dry well. Thomas Wayne asks him, "Why do we fall, Bruce? So we can learn to pick ourselves up." Striving for success does not exempt us from failure. Many failures have knocked me down. I've come up short on many goals. One of my professional goals was to get my PMP (Project Management Professional) certification. I believed I was ready. Within my role at automotive company, I was a project manager.

After applying, I gathered the resources to study. Experience may not be enough without key fundamentals. Experience and studying didn't yield a certification. I failed the test. Didn't even score above average in any of the five knowledge areas. This disappointing setback led me to believe I wasn't qualified enough. The project management institute allows you to take the test up to three times during one calendar year. Taking the test is an investment. The real test is harder than the practice test. It was a tricky multiple-choice test. My kryptonite of not being a good test taker got the best of me. My confidence was shaken, and I couldn't find the courage to take the test again.

Certifications can enhance your professional portfolio. They give you credibility. They showcase your niche. I wanted to stand out in a world full of engineers. Commitment to your craft will speak volumes. Certifications can boost salary. Use them as a way to advocate for a raise. Determination will get you to the goal. Being resilient is what determines whether we fight through it, grow through it, or cave in and let these challenges defeat us. Your capacity to recover from difficulties is vital.

Things will not get any easier, but one must become stronger. Often we fail and agonize over it. We question the why and the how. Failure is another teacher in life. Learn to accept the loss and embrace the lesson it teaches you. With some failures you will get up more quickly than others. It has taken me two years to re-commit myself to PMP. Last time, I tried to do everything on my own. I did some research and put together a different plan. It cost me more money, but the return on investment will be worth it. Never lose heart. Hang on to faith. Be resilient.

Your character is what gives people insight into who you are. It's what you stand for. Within character lies **integrity**, a core value that must guide you in decision making. In life we must abide by a code of ethics. It's called the law. In businesses there are ethical and compliance measures in place. Corporate ethics courses give you a foundation. They teach employees what is right and wrong in handling corporate affairs. In reality there are instances when doing what is right gets overshadowed due to pressure. Organizations will do just about anything to outperform competition. The "YES" (wo)man will bend, going against the norm, if it furthers their career.

<u>Case Scenario I</u>

In 2017, Phillip Lee Terry was crushed to death by a forklift while working at an Amazon facility. The state investigator concluded that Amazon was at fault. The company was cited four major safety violations and fined $28,000. What's $28,000 to a billion-dollar company? Amazon appealed the citations and fines. This incident was a big deal for the city of Indianapolis. Unfortunately people do die on the job. The issue of this man's death was the timing. Amazon had started a statewide campaign and initiative to build a new company headquarters outside of Seattle. Indianapolis was one of the twenty finalists. In a report it was revealed state officials overturned the citations to lure Amazon's headquarters to Indiana.

The blame shifted to the maintenance worker Phillip Lee Terry. The victim was held responsible for his own death. Conflict had arisen from the state investigator report, which claimed Amazon was at fault due to lack of safety culture and training. Per reports, the state investigator was pressured and told to back off. Allegedly Indiana OSHA's director colluded with an Amazon official to shift the blame to employee misconduct. The OSHA director mentioned to the investigator on manipulating citations. John Stallone, the state's investigator, was given two options. Back off or resign. John chose the latter. Indiana did not end up being chosen for the new headquarters.

There are two sides to every story. Mr. Terry is no longer here to tell his side on what led up to the forklift malfunction. The lesson within this case is ethics and moral value principles. You will be involved in projects and situations that will test your integrity. Taking a stand for what is right can cost you your job or career. At the end of the day, you have to answer for all the things you did in life, good and bad. Ethics is subjective. What may hold true for one person is not the case for another. You will have to evaluate your own moral principles against the ethics. I always ask myself what there is to gain. On the flip side, what is there to lose?

Seek truth and nothing but the truth. Individuals have not always liked what I had to say, but they highly respected me because of my honesty. My third month working at automotive company, I got sent to Mexico with my boss. At dinner a Mexican colleague asked me questions pertaining to my boss. I gave honest answers. I will never forget his advice to me: "just lie." I will never blur the truth just to make another (wo)man feel better about themselves. I've accepted the fact that it could hold me back in some ways. I am a woman of integrity.

Case Scenario II

Boeing is under fire by FAA. Their 737 MAX jets have resulted in two fatal plane crashes. Prior to the crashes, Boeing knew about concerns raised by two employees. There is documentation of conversations within the company on the aircraft. All the facts are not known. FAA has not reported on when the issues arose. Many companies have risk mitigation plans. As part of governance, a proposed plan is needed. Members of the committee vote on whether the risks have been addressed to move on to the next phase of the project. Politics and bureaucracy can take over and rule against governance.

Individuals turn a deaf ear to issues. Nobody wants

to hear the truth. It takes too long to work out and more time is required. Is it worth it when more than three hundred lives have been lost? When others fall in integrity, you must stand. Always have the documentation to back you up. Your integrity will be tested. I led continuous improvement meetings at my paint company. There were some details getting left in the dark. It had caught up with us. I had been asked to review and change some documentation. There were lots of high action items. My message to the team was to trust the work and the criteria we used to come to this agreement. It's a bad look on business to not have it together. The purpose of a PFMEA was to drive improvements. I told my colleague, you can change the document. The story that was told was not accurate. It came back to haunt us.

Many have sight, very few have vision. **Vision** is the ability to think about or plan for the future with imagination and wisdom. The vision you have for your life is your guiding light. It will order your steps. When there are bumps in the road, it will be your motivation to keep going. Greatness is achieved through creative power. It can be constructed through vision boards and vision statements.

The NSBE professional development conference

hosts an executive leadership roundtable forum that introduces the audience to executives in their perspective industries. You hear the journeys on how to navigate your career to the C-suite. The one thing they had in common was each executive had a vision statement. Journals were given to attendees. They asked us to write our own personal vision statement. This requires a deeper level of reflection. Don't write it and forget it. As you grow, your vision may change. You may have multiple visions for your personal life and your professional life. My vision statement reads:

My life journey is to make a difference. My goal is to impact the world through motivational and educational presentations. My vision is to educate, empower, and elevate those who I am called to serve. Educating audiences on the history of who they are, where they come from, and knowledge to move them forward. Empowering people beyond the trials and tribulations to overcome. The reason I wrote this book stems from this.

Poster board and magazines are all you need to create a vision board. Habakkuk 2:2 tells us to write the vision down and make it plain on tablets, so that a herald may run with it.

We are not human beings having a spiritual experience; we are spiritual beings having a human experience. People are imperfect. Nobody gets it right 100 percent of the time. Continuing to reach your highest potential requires you to strive for **excellence**. NBA executive Pat Riley says excellence is the gradual result of always striving to do better. Every day I wake up and ask, What can I do today to be better? Excellence is the building block to greatness. Create a roadmap for your development. Embodying the D.R.I.V.E. characteristics of determination, resilience, integrity, vision, and excellence, there is no telling what you will achieve. Stay driven on your path.

Chapter 8

Mastering Skills to Achieve Excellence

One of life's biggest questions is, What are the keys to being successful? Looking back on the previous chapter, those five characteristics are the foundation for success. Along with characteristics, one needs skills. Skills enable you to do something well. In doing well, you level up to achieving excellence. The two skills you must master are communication and leadership.

Failure to communicate well will not take you far. I used to never speak up in meetings. I was afraid. Public speaking was frightening to me. Speaking puts all the attention on you. As an introvert, it can be uncomfortable.

The speaker of the moment is open to criticism. Being put in a position of leading projects, I knew I had to overcome my fears. I didn't want to be labeled and put in a box. "Although Brittany is a hardworking engineer, she fails to communicate; why should she advance?" I never heard this, but I didn't want that narrative to play out. When I first started leading meetings, my communication was terrible. My boss told me that I talked too fast. Nobody could understand what I was saying.

Others told me there were certain words that I said constantly, such as "you know" and "um." My first gate review I read off a sheet of paper. My boss said, "Anybody can do that." There was a lot more room with constructive criticism. The more meetings I ran, the better my communication got. Communication requires practice. Preparing for meetings in advance is helpful. It enabled me to walk through the slides and create the story around them. When it was my day to present, I was more in control.

My boss could tell the difference. He said, "You have definitely gotten better." I was advised to continue honing my speaking skills. My recommendation for you is to join Toastmasters, an organization comprised of clubs worldwide. The purpose of these clubs is to promote communication, public speaking, and leadership. In the club meetings, you practice giving prepared and impromptu speeches ("table talks"). When I moved to Indianapolis, I started attending the local Toastmaster club. I gave a talk on my first day about the worst vacation I ever had.

I got up, spoke, and left that meeting with a ribbon for Best Table Topic. I gave another speech on a concert I went to. I had the room laughing. Feedback was beneficial. My confidence was high. It gave me validation that I could do this in a corporate setting, too. Communication is more than just words. Recall my example with my colleague learning to communicate through presentation. To communicate well, you must know your audience.

During a professional development workshop, code switching was introduced to me. Code switching means identifying your personality style and knowing when to adapt to others. Being detail-oriented is part of my personality. As engineers, we want the details and facts before moving forward. In turn, we present information laid out in detail. There are those personalities who are data-driven. Skip giving them the story and state key performance metrics. It would be helpful as a team exercise to know everyone's personality style. This is unlikely to happen.

Careful attention must be paid to teach the people you are involved with. To become an effective communicator, learn more than one language. The science and engineering enterprise is a global market. Business is done all across the world. You don't have to become fluent, but knowing at least some of another language or two will aid in your own personal and professional development. If I could go back, I would have taken language courses in college. Duolingo is a very effective app for learning language. It goes wherever you go. As the learner, you can set your own time limit and goal.

Gaining an understanding of some basic words will help you build the foundation. Some Americans think everyone should speak English. Due to accents and dialects, the context of the conversation may not always be understood. Try to meet diverse teams in the middle. Work together to create a system of communication. I've been in meetings where both English and Spanish were used. Part of the meeting was talking about process flow. The technical details got translated into Spanish for the Mexico team. As details were being explained, I wrote down key words in English and then Spanish. In recapping key details, I then said the Spanish words.

Being an effective communicator takes work.

Casa El Rey Moro Museum is located in San Diego, California. The museum is owned and operated by Chuck Ambers. He is a walking encyclopedia of black history. Professor Ambers asked me how many languages I spoke. He said that if you can only function in one language, it controls your mind. One technique that I've used to help me communicate is speaking out loud over a voice memo. Tap your microphone and randomly start talking about a topic. Don't focus on the length, but quality. After the recording I analyze my speech pattern.

Tone of voice: Is the talk engaging or does it sound like I am putting people to sleep?

Speed of words: Am I talking too fast or too slow?

Speech pattern: Do I circle around my words and often say "um," "like," and "so"?

The self-audit is helpful to evaluate ways I can do better next time. You can learn by watching and observing others. Leaders are required to give communication meetings to employees. During one meeting, an executive said "um" every other word. The piece of paper shook in his hand. The plant employees were numb to his message. It was an hour to daydream because people found it difficult to pay attention. It's not easy getting up in front of a room to talk. It can be nerve- racking.

The lesson learned from him was engagement: how (not) to hold audience attention. One tool he didn't utilize was PowerPoint. Elimination of the notepad in hand would take away the distraction of his hands shaking. No more than five bullet points and same graphics. PowerPoint should aid in telling the story. Practice to reduce nervousness, but not so much it makes you seem robotic. Studying the art of communication is a system. Define your inputs to the system. What works for you as a communicator? Study the art of communication by watching great orators.

Review what people say about the speaker. Communicating well comes from within. Self-confidence is required. Often your message may not resonate with your audience. This is OK! Take the feedback and build upon it. My continuous improvement presentation got ripped apart during a process engineering roundtable meeting. I took the criticism and noted how to be better next time. Continuous improvement is about what we are planning to do in the future. My presentation didn't include low-hanging fruit. The manager wanted this information. I had failed to connect the past to the future on how KPI's (Key Performance Indicators) would be improved. Keep at it and your competency and skills of communicating will grow.

Climbing the corporate ladder is the ultimate goal for some. Many believe this is where leadership begins. The position of authority and influence is now at their discretion. The assumption is the title of president, director, or vice-president validates leadership. But some of the best leaders are not in the C-suite. How can one lead at the top if they have not learned to lead at the bottom?

Leadership is a key skill to achieving one's own excellence. There are many different types of leaders. I've experienced the political leader, the narcissist leader, the dictatorship leader, and the insecure leader. Having examples of leadership styles has developed my leadership abilities. The one thing that held me back was believing leadership begins at the top. If everybody leads at the top, who is leading at the bottom or in the middle? My mindset shifted after reading John C, Maxwell's *The 360-Degree Leader.*

Imagine just boarding a flight and taking off to your destination. While the plane is on the ground, you observe the loading of luggage, providing fuel to the plane, and the signal to begin taxiing from the gate. At the takeoff point, you begin to rise into the sky. The things you observed on the ground shrink. As you climb in altitude, you no longer have that view of the runway, highway, or houses. Everything is at a bird's-eye view. You are not aware of what is taking place because the plane is at 35,000 feet.

The C-suite is similar. Leaders at the top lose sight of the reality of the interworking of the business. They have the slightest clue what's going on. Granted, they get reports sent up to them. It's crowded at the top. So the rest fall down within the trenches. Although many get to the C-suite faster than others, it's a long climb. I've learned to lead from the middle. My role was within the middle of the organization. I utilized my skills, abilities, and knowledge to do the "little" things that influence the bigger picture. No matter what level, leadership requires work.

One misconception people have is that being a boss makes you a leader. Far from the truth. Self-reflection required me to define the type of leader I wanted to be. Should I imitate the leadership I'd been accustomed to? My first job in college was working at the university bookstore. It was HELL! The director's leadership style was one of a dictator. His way was the only way. Students working in the bookstore were not allowed to sit down unless we were on a break. This made sense if the store was full of people. During our non-busy time, this made no sense. The floor was concrete. To stand for six to eight hours was hard on the body even for a young person.

There was no fun. You couldn't laugh, joke, or really talk. He didn't want employees talking. A no-homework policy was established, even when the store had no customers. I went to work some days and did NOTHING. The bookstore had a high turnover of employees. Being young adults, we understood there are rules to follow. This system was just insane. He never talked to the workers. Just sat in his office and overlooked the store. The solution to get workers to stay was higher pay. This didn't work. In exit interviews, people would say he was the reason for quitting.

It's not good to have a bad attitude every day. You could sense it among us. Work culture should inspire togetherness. We worked in isolation handling our tasks. I am about business. I'd want people to enjoy working. It's OK to be free and engage colleagues. If this is not allowed, how can there be teamwork toward a common goal? Never would these type of leadership qualities be adopted in my philosophy.

Politicians campaign for the vote of the people. They promise tax breaks for all. All talk and no action. Many are in the race for their own personal gain. Corporate America is full of politician-style leaders. Working under this type of leader puts insurmountable pressure to hit home runs. Innovation is part of research and development. Managers must have a vision for it. It has to be communicated where design development can begin. Up to bat, a homerun is expected. Let's be more methodical and swing to get on base first. At times we tend to bite off more than we can chew. Managers are unbothered by this, because they are not the ones who have to deliver. Requirements and guidelines help engineers solve problems. Being political worked for my manager because he got where he wanted to be.

My former boss was promoted to eight-level executive, a very high career promotion for a manager. He had fallen out of favor with his people. Many didn't value his thought leadership. It just didn't exist. Talking that talk was all noise. Team members tuned him out in meetings. He attempted to inspire us in one meeting. He talked about right-turn innovation. This concept was developed by UPS. UPS routes are set up so the driver never takes a left turn. The company is efficient in saving time and money, leading to more profitability. In advanced development, how can we make right turns? This is where it ended. No applicability to how this applied to the automotive industry. One engineer even asked, what does this mean for us? Think of other ways to innovate, John replied. But vision should start with the leader.

All individuals should read. Read beyond the Google search engine. Reading is fundamental and provokes thought leadership. As a thought leader, you inspire people with innovative ideas, provide strategic plans to turn ideas into reality, and know what it takes to be successful.

Don't make it all about you. If it's just about you, then you're the narcissist leader: self-ambition, lacking empathy, believing others are inferior to you. When you have this type of leader, no one can share the spotlight. They are the spotlight. I'd been chosen to be the ambassador for cultural transformation at our plant. As the ambassador, I was assigned to train others on a corporate-wide initiative. Each plant was to roll out the initiative. A decision was made to incorporate plant management. Together we were to teach the team. First, I was left out of the meetings. Second, plant managers decided they were going to do it. Time and money were wasted for me to travel to Texas. Training was a disaster.

Trainers couldn't hold the audience's attention and lost control of the meeting. To get the best out of people, you don't belittle their intelligence. Individuals may not be equipped to perform all tasks. This is a reason for training and development. Only look down on someone to uplift them.

Define your leadership style. Leadership is a gift that must be unwrapped from within. In principle, it shouldn't be about hovering over people, but serving those you lead. Personalities may define how one leads. One of my spiritual gifts is encouragement. No matter what is discussed, I aim to end the conversation on a positive note. My method for managing teams is neither dominant nor meek. Behavioral attitudes must be addressed. People will not always do the job right. The project leader must address the conflict.

Skilled trades are the heart and soul of manufacturing. I value their work ethic, especially in crunch time. Efficiency in building too fast can be counterproductive to quality. With serious issues arising, the talk had to be given on the technicians building quality. My leadership approach to giving criticism is the sandwich method. I learned this method of communication during my time at financial services. It begins with a level of appreciation for what they have done. The "meat" of the message is constructive criticism. Stated as "Although there is quota to meet, I prefer quality over quantity. Think about what we are building. How we are building it. Building requires pace and rhythm, but don't let it become robotic."

Keep up the good work ethic and if I can provide anything that makes your job easier, let me know. 100 good parts is better than 500 bad parts. If we can't build good parts in regular work hours, we will not build them on overtime hours. Very few leaders respect those who work for them. In order for the business to succeed, there has to be respect both ways. Developing and cultivating relationships is part of the job. As leaders, we should not muzzle an ox while it's threshing. Establish values. Lead by the values. Guiding principles help drive the mission forward. In times of difficulty, they are there for you to lean on.

Values helps build a framework for team success. The framework should include P.A.T.: Passion, Accountability, and Transparency. Create the systems and processes where values are embedded, where cohesiveness grows the team together. I value accountability. Employees are responsible to complete tasks and perform duties. I hold myself responsible to lead and govern teams. Project work requires actions to get fulfilled. In leading project teams, I created an open-issues tracker. This is my system for holding key members accountable, an open dialogue spreadsheet that creates discussion on the work needing to be done.

I operate off passion. No one wants to follow an uncommitted person. I haven't always gotten the best assignments. Anything I have ever done was done with passion. Passion energizes teams. It fuels desire. Desire lights the path to success. We tell people what they want to hear. Transparency is often underappreciated. I am not in the business of selling false hope and lies. You will see this in your career. Key Performance Indicator metrics is often where transparency goes out the door. Metrics can be an illusion. People are aiming to achieve false narratives. No individual wants to come out and say we are failing. The first reason is it may cause panic. The second reason is you may lose trust. You will continue to dig a hole for yourself that is too deep to climb out of.

No matter where you may fall on the leadership scale, develop your business acumen. When I worked in automotive, I took business acumen training. The basics of the training was understanding how businesses make money. How to read a financial analysis and interpret it.

Understanding how executives make decisions. From our position in the organization we could make better decisions that align with corporate objectives. To rise to the top, you must first show what impact you have on the bottom. Learn to do the small things well. Focus on doing what matters, instead of what will get you noticed. Your time will come. When it does, be prepared to take on the challenge.

The best project you will ever work on or lead is YOU! Leadership is not just tied to position, title, or assignment. It takes being a servant follower to become a servant leader.

Tips for leadership

- Prepare Each Day

- Commit to the Process

- TAP into your values

- Listen more than you speak

- Bring something to the table

- Learn to lead from where you are

Mastering skills to achieve excellence is more of an art than a science. Experience has been my teacher.

Utilize your own experiences and intuition to build your professional platform.

Chapter 9

Believing in YOU!

Self-doubt is the biggest detriment to success. It kills the human spirit. Hope is choked off. Faith in yourself has to be greater than the opposition within you. The road to science and engineering is full of trials and tribulations. Just know that many were on this same path before you. Your ancestors ran the race to pass the baton to YOU. Take it and run. And, in turn, future generations are depending on you to show them the way. The word need your brilliance to continue to engineer the world around us

You may question whether it is for you. Yes, STEM is for you. Will you be for it?

Believe you are more than just a statistic.

Believe that you are meant for a greater purpose than yourself.

Believe you will succeed. Never doubt the route God is taking you on. For He knows the plans he has for you, plans to prosper you, plans to give you hope and a future. The ones who believe they can will be the ones who do. I wouldn't have written this book if I didn't believe you couldn't. I look forward to your journey. Your mission will empower others. They will one day stand on your shoulders.

Epilogue

"The dream is free, but the hustle is sold separately."
George GK Koufalis

For ten years, I have dreamed of writing these letters to you. Self-doubt, life, and fear has been in my way. There are already books out in the marketplace addressing the need for more female engineers. I made the excuse of letting "others" do the work. Got complacent in my goals because I had made it out of Youngstown and I started earning a lot more money. I began traveling and spending my time elsewhere.

It was through meditation that I realized I was not fulfilling my calling. Even then I doubted if I was qualified. God doesn't call the qualified. He qualifies those he has called. That's when I knew it was time to shine light on my people. I am not called to inspire the masses. Realistically we won't inspire every woman in the world to become an engineer. If I can help one young woman reach her potential, then I know I have fulfilled the call.

People continue to ask me, "Brittany, what is it going to take to get more young girls interested in STEM?" I reply it's my dream to see more women fill the pipeline. Again, you do not get what you wish for. Dreams have to be backed up by action. That's when I knew I had to share the power of my perspective. This book will only reinforce the mission. It's my way of making a difference and engineering the world around me! Meeting the needs of America's next technical workforce. I hope that one day we will both be sitting at the table together.

Resource Guide

This resource guide contains a list of books that have helped me learn about my culture, developed me as a leader, and provided a strategy for me to navigate my career.

I. Learning

- *Africa Counts,* by Claudia Zaslavsky

- *Black Women Scientists in the United States,* by Wini Warren

- *Blacks in Science,* by Ivan Van Sertima

- *The Story of the Moors in Spain,* by Stanley Lane-Poole

II. Development

- *Developing the Leader Within You,* by John C. Maxwell

- *The 360 Degree Leader,* by John C. Maxwell

- *Seeing the Big Picture,* by Kevin Cope

- *The Sharp Solution,* by Heidi Hanna

III. **Strategy**

- *Hardball for Women,* by Pat Heim and Tammy Hughes, with Susan K. Golant

- *Successful Women Think Differently,* by Valorie Burton

- *Never Split the Difference,* by Chris Voss

- *Guaranteed 4.0,* by Donna O. Johnson